Special Needs in the Early Years

Collaboration, communication and coordination

Second Edition

Sue Roffey

David Fulton Publishers

London

David Fulton Publishers Ltd
Ormond House, 26–27 Boswell Street, London WC1N 3JZ

First published in Great Britain by David Fulton Publishers 1999
Reprinted 2000
Second edition published 2001

British Library Cataloguing in Publication Data
A catalogue record for this book is available from the British Library

ISBN 1–85346–759–6

Typeset by FiSH Books, London
Printed in Great Britain by The Cromwell Press Ltd, Trowbridge, Wilts.

Contents

Preface

Ideally, services for children with special needs and their families would be provided as a result of joint planning at every level. Although it is acknowledged that families often do receive a fragmented service there is currently a determination from many quarters to improve service delivery. The themes of this book have now become centre stage, both in terms of collaborative structures and pooled funding. Since the first edition there have been several initiatives from the Government to promote joint working such as *Working Together to Safeguard Children* (DOH, DfEE and Home Office 1999) which sets out guidelines for inter-agency coordination to promote the welfare of children. There is also greater emphasis in the SEN Code of Practice 2001 on working in partnership with other agencies. This increasing recognition of good collaborative practice for children and families which happens in some areas needs to develop nationwide and be taken on board at the most senior levels of management.

There are many hurdles implicit in this aim and, although these issues are discussed, the main focus here is the promotion of effective communication and collaboration which helps to ensure that a child's needs are met in early years settings, particularly in partnership with parents. There is a focus on inclusive practices and the needs of teachers and nursery officers in mainstream provision who may be less experienced in working with young children with special educational needs and their parents. This book is intended to be a resource that will:

- clarify the contexts in which people are working
- clarify the roles that different professionals may have
- raise issues related to communication with parents and others
- provide a framework for joint planning

- explore ways of strengthening in-school communication and collaboration
- give examples of good practice which might be replicated or adapted.

This book covers the range and continuum of special educational needs, from those that are complex and require substantive intervention throughout a child's early years and education to those which are mild or temporary. 'Early years' within the context of this book follows the Children Act definition, which is from birth to eight years.

Note: The use of the pronouns 'he' and 'she' for children are used in alternative chapters, with the exception of Chapter Five which alternates throughout. The definition of 'parent' includes all those who have a legal or practical responsibility for the child's care and welfare. Where teachers are mentioned this also refers to any professional working within a pre-school setting or infant school. Similarly, 'school' or 'nursery' refers to all early years educational provision. This book is substantially based on the SEN Code of Practice draft for consultation (2000). Any variation between the draft and the final version will be incorporated at the first reprint.

Sue Roffey
Sydney
June 2001

Acknowledgements

Many people gave generously of their time by talking with me, providing guidance on specific issues, directing me to sources of information or reading drafts of the manuscript. Some parents of young children with special educational needs also shared their experiences with me. I am grateful to the following:

Joan Armstrong, Mog Ball, John Bissett, Cyndy Bowles, Lorraine Clarke, Kairen Cullen, Sarah Dean, Roy Earnshaw, Jane Elias, Shelley Flain, Elizabeth Gillies, Maria Greenwood, Julian Grenier, Ed Hook, Helen Horton, Margaret Hollinghurst, Jane Knowles, Michele Lindsay, Karen Majors, Ben Marshall, Jackie Martin, Hannah Mortimer, Jill Murphy, Hannah Murphy, Philip Peatfield, Marion Porter, Anita Robinson, Anne Robinson, Judy Roux, David Rubra, Calie Shearer, Bernadette Simpson, Caroline Smith, Frank Smith, Sheila Smith, Kay Tisdall, Geraldine Trussman, Helen Warburton, Michele Ward, Carole Warden, Dawn Weaver, Mary Welsh, Sheila Wolfendale and Caroline Woollett. I would also like to thank Alison Foyle (formerly of David Fulton Publishers), Jude Bowen and the other helpful staff at David Fulton Publishers.

Thanks are especially due to Nic Watts who provided the illustrations, and to Emily Perl Kingsley for permission to reproduce *Welcome to Holland* (p.8).

My family yet again came up trumps with the necessary support and encouragement, and my partner David helped to keep me on reasonably good terms with the word processor throughout.

Sue Roffey has many years experience as a teacher and an educational psychologist. She is currently based in Australia where she is attached to the University of Western Sydney. Sue works as a researcher and consultant on emotional, social and behavioural issues in education and has written widely on these topics. She is a founder member of ESIA, a network promoting emotional literacy in Australia.

Sue provides professional development and training in both Australia and the UK. She can be contacted at sue@sueroffey.com

For Bettina Rallison

CHAPTER 1

Introduction

This book is about one of the most crucial factors in special education – effective and empathetic communication.

Good communication, especially in the early years, is of vital importance, and can make a significant difference to children, their families and those working with them. It is essential both to ensure clarity of aims and continuity of progress for the child and to promote confidence in parents and teachers in meeting children's needs. Good communication is about sharing aims, participation in decision making, planning, reviewing and making the best use of resources. It is also about reassurance.

How communication takes place is as important as the content. It has a significant impact on what is heard and ultimately what happens for each individual child. We are therefore concerned here about both the content and the process of communication, how information is shared taking account of contexts and especially the facilitation of partnership with parents.

'It takes a village'

The much-quoted African proverb 'It takes a village to raise a child' is especially true when it comes to children with special educational needs (SEN). In Britain today, especially in urban areas, this 'village' is not so much a group of neighbours as a whole community of professionals, advisers, teachers and other workers who may be required to support the family's efforts and help the child to make optimum progress.

Sometimes a child's special needs are evident at or soon after birth. For many other families, the realisation that their child has a difficulty in one or more areas of development dawns slowly. Whichever is the case, the child's needs will become the focus for a number of adults who have a range of views, concerns and priorities. These individuals will come from some or all of the following groups:

- the parents and immediate family
- extended family and close friends
- others who will be caring for the child at home, nursery or playgroup
- medical or paramedical professionals such as health visitors, doctors, speech therapists and physiotherapists
- educational professionals such as teachers, pre-school coordinators, educational psychologists (EPs) and education support services
- Social Services personnel, who may include specialist social workers, day care officers, workers in respite or holiday schemes
- other support services such as home support services (e.g. portage workers), an independent parental support worker in a Parent Partnership Scheme
- voluntary agencies
- special needs administrative officers within local education authorities (LEAs).

The child is part of a number of different systems, in which she lives and learns (see Figure 1.1). She is part of a family network, part of an education system, and a direct user of the Health Services. She may also be a direct or indirect user of Social Services. These systems overlap and interact at given points and at certain times. Some individuals in these systems are close to the child and may be in contact on a daily basis. Others are more peripheral but nevertheless exert an influence on what happens for the child as they are linked in some way to the systems and the people who support the child's development.

The various people involved form part of a wider system and, whether they realise it or not, each affects the other. When something happens in one part of the system, there will be shifts elsewhere. A mother who feels supported may have more emotional energy to interact positively with her child who may in turn respond more readily, and may make more progress as a result. A family who have felt uncomfortable with one professional may be more wary of the next one they come into contact with and there will be barriers to communication which again may have consequences all down the line. An early years worker who has fully understood what a physiotherapist has advised, and has felt able to clarify any uncertainties in a meeting, will be more skilled in adapting the environment appropriately for the child. The expectations and influence of a member of the extended family may influence how a parent sees his child, and this in turn affects how he perceives the advice given to him.

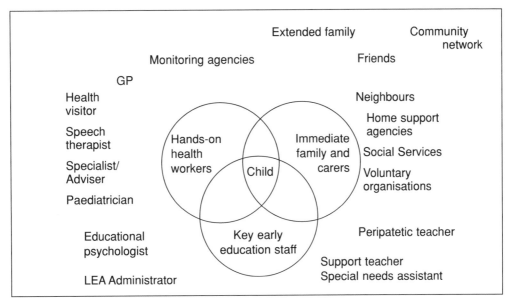

Figure 1.1 'The child is part of a number of different systems . . .'

Roles and responsibilities

Although all of these individuals would say that they want the best for the child in question, each has his or her own perspectives and priorities. They all have different roles and responsibilities and are operating within different contexts. Some are involved in order to make a particular kind of assessment and offer advice, others to work with the child to promote development; some will be more concerned with monitoring progress, others with supporting the family. Some, especially teachers, will see the child as one of many; whereas for the parent the child is the priority – but also part of the wider family. Some of these roles are multiple, others overlap and sometimes it may not be entirely clear who is supposed to be doing what.

It takes a determined effort to develop this potentially disparate and fragmented group of individuals into a cooperative team, who are able to communicate effectively with each other to meet the needs of the whole child within the context of her whole family and in a whole class group. The fact that traditionally professionals come from different disciplines, which have different organisational structures and different funding arrangements, has not helped. In many places, geographical boundaries are not in alignment and there is a need to work across local authorities. People may not know about the context in which other colleagues are working, and even the definitions used may be different. Some people, particularly in the Health Services, may see the child as having an innate problem that requires 'treatment', whereas many other professionals in Education and Social Services have a more interactive perspective.

'Working together' is seen as a much-valued concept in the literature and in the legislation but the reality is plagued with difficulties and there is a wide range of practice across the country. Many parents find themselves in the position of passing information around, sometimes at a time when they may themselves feel confused and unclear. Sometimes their confusion is exacerbated by the different information that they receive from different professionals.

Since the Children Act 1989 (DOH 1991) and the Code of Practice for SEN (DfEE 1994), together with the SEN Code of Practice published in 2001, there has been a greater effort to organise things differently to promote a higher level of collaboration. This has been emphasised even further with the introduction of Early Years Development and Childcare Partnerships and Working Together to Safeguard Children. Much good practice, however, appears to depend on individuals who are deeply committed to the principle of inter-agency cooperation and many schemes are still in the early stages of development. Examples of good practice are given throughout the book. The legal framework is summarised in Chapter 2, and Chapter 3 gives a more detailed explanation of professional responsibilities within different disciplines.

Levels of knowledge and confidence

An important difference between these groups concerned with the child is the type and level of knowledge they possess about a child's particular needs, about the child within the family and about SEN procedures and resources. Knowledge gives rise both to confidence about what might be done to promote development and to appropriate expectations. Parents and carers may begin by knowing very little about their child's particular special needs but over time may become more knowledgeable than anyone else. In the early years, however, the plethora of assessment, advice and suggestion from many different concerned sources may only add to the feelings of anxiety, frustration, guilt and confusion that often beset a family who are learning to come to terms with and manage their child's special needs.

With the increased focus on providing a mainstream experience for children with SEN and including them in many of the activities and experiences that are open to others of the same age, more adults in early years settings are coming into contact with children who have a range of needs. In the same way that parents may be more or less knowledgeable and confident, this is also true for nursery officers and early years teachers. Where people are clearer about what is expected of them, and feel that they have the resources or support to do what might be required, it is easier for them to welcome children and their families warmly and positively.

With the family's agreement, it is also helpful if knowledge is shared about the whole child and the contexts in which she both lives and learns. A chance remark or suggestion, which shows little understanding about demands on the family or special needs procedures, can serve to increase guilt or raise unrealistic expectations that may generate frustration and conflict.

Development, progress and change

Any child's needs and development do not remain static and, especially in the early years, can change considerably over a few months. Good communication enhances continuity, especially during transition periods and when new people become involved. Chapter 6 is concerned with aspects of communication and liaison within a school or nursery. It also looks at what needs to happen when children move on. Good, regular, liaison ensures there will be a consistency of approach, evaluation of intervention, updated programmes, and that any new information is shared and taken into account when planning.

As some children with SEN may make very few steps over a review period of several weeks or even months, it is important that people hold on to the progress that children are in fact making. It is worthwhile to look back sometimes on progress made over longer periods so that everyone can be reminded of the results of their efforts. The annual review process for Statemented children is supposed to do this but sometimes gets lost in the enthusiasm to plan forward rather than look back.

The importance of early intervention

All the recent legislation and guidance on children's SEN puts a firm emphasis on the importance of early intervention. There are some obvious reasons for this and others which are more subtle but equally important.

Promoting development

The more obvious reason for early intervention is that the earlier a child's needs are addressed and, where appropriate, programmes put into place, then the more progress the child is likely to make. Babies and small children, especially in the pre-school years, are at their most responsive and flexible, their brains more able to adapt to new ways of working. The younger a child is when intervention begins, the more chance there will be of making optimum progress – so long as the programme which is devised is appropriate for her developmental stage and suitable for her needs.

It is very important that the child is seen as a whole person and each area of her development is given attention. Where the child's difficulties and her remediation are the overwhelming focus for the entire family there is a danger that normal elements of functioning are ignored, possibly with negative consequences for the child's well-being in other areas. Collaboration and communication between parents, teachers and professionals will not only help to identify intervention, but also ensure that the child's needs are seen in the context of her overall development.

Maintaining the child's self-esteem

Self-esteem is not always the first thing that people think of when considering the importance of early intervention. When a child has inappropriate demands made on her, however, and experiences failure on a regular basis she may develop a self-concept of herself as someone who 'can't' or 'is lazy' or who causes her parents distress. The child who experiences continual failure will eventually be reluctant to try and this will impede her progress even further. The earlier there is a good understanding of the child's difficulties and needs, the earlier there will be appropriate expectations and celebration of success when these are achieved. At the opposite end of the spectrum some parents are so protective of their child they do everything for her. These expectations are equally inappropriate and do not encourage the child to try things for herself and develop optimum independence.

Supporting parents

Emotional support

Much has been written about working in partnership with parents, but it is in these early days when a child's SEN are first identified that the interactions between the family and others are at their most crucial. The experience of having to face the reality that your child may in some way be different from others is potentially devastating. There is some evidence to indicate that not all parents have been told this news with the sensitivity that the situation requires (Herbert 1994).

Many families go through what can only be described as a period of grief. Like a bereavement, parents may go through stages of denial, shock, anger, guilt, overwhelming sadness and even depression before they are able to accept the reality of their child's special needs. For some families that point never really comes. The professionals who come into contact with parents, especially in the early days, may face some of these emotional responses and need to be prepared for them. Initial approaches to parents make a difference to how they view the professionals they will meet in the future. What is said to parents at this time also impinges on their feelings about themselves and their child. These include feelings of guilt that so often accompany having a child with difficulties, their anxieties about the future for their child and how she will manage and the future for themselves and how they will cope. There are also likely to be concerns about effects on the rest of the family.

Finding the right balance between acknowledgement of the parents' emotional response, the reality of the situation and being positive about the possibilities is not easy. The Royal National Institute for the Blind (RNIB) has published guidance for professionals about the way information is given (specifically for blind or partially sighted children) which includes the timing of this, the amount of information to give and the support parents need. Detailed and summary versions are available from the RNIB. Much of the advice is applicable to a range of SEN.

The strength of the support network for carers may be linked to the progress the child makes. Parents who can go to others who will listen, accept their child, not be judgemental, and offer advice and guidance when it is asked for may be better able to come to terms with what has happened and forge a more positive relationship with their child. Often this support network includes the professionals with whom the parent comes into contact, as well as the extended family, voluntary groups and other families. In some cases, it may be the entire support network the parent has.

It is important to remember that parents often have many other demands on them. The child who is the focus for the professionals is only one of a family's concerns and parents may worry about the effects on their other children. Working 'with' parents means being able to take into consideration not only what it is possible for them to do but also what is feasible. Unless parents are truly part of the decision making process they may agree to something that is in effect unrealistic. This may only serve to increase the guilt they may already be feeling and put further demands on an already overstretched family.

Figure 1.2 is a vivid analogy given by a parent to illustrate how it felt for her to have to come to terms with having a child with complex special needs.

Welcome to Holland
by Emily Perl Kingsley

I am often asked to describe the experience of raising a child with a disability – to try to help people who have not shared that unique experience to understand it, to imagine how it would feel. It's like this …

When you are going to have a baby, it's like planning a fabulous vacation trip – to Italy. You buy a bunch of guidebooks and make your wonderful plans. The Coliseum. The Michelangelo David. The gondolas in Venice. You may learn some handy phrases in Italian. It's all very exciting.

After months of eager anticipation, the day finally arrives. You pack your bags and off you go. Several hours later, the plane lands. The stewardess comes in and says, 'Welcome to Holland.'

'Holland?!?' you say. 'What do you mean Holland?? I signed up for Italy! I'm supposed to be in Italy. All my life I've dreamed of going to Italy.' But there's been a change in the flight plan. They've landed in Holland and there you must stay.

The important thing is that they haven't taken you to a horrible, disgusting, filthy place, full of pestilence, famine and disease. It's just a different place.

So you must go out and buy new guidebooks. And you must learn a whole new language. And you will meet a whole new group of people you would never have met.

CHAPTER 2

The Legal Context

The people who work on behalf of young children with SEN do so within a complex framework of legislation and guidance. Although everyone must take note of all the legislation, the emphasis for them all will depend on their particular profession and who employs them. In general teachers will work within the SEN Code of Practice 2001 guidelines for SEN (DfEE 2001; Circular 4/96 in Scotland, SOEID 1996), social workers and the health professionals within Children's Service Plans and pre-school providers with Early Years Development and Childcare Plans. There are increasing expectations that plans will be integrated with each other and be developed in partnership to provide seamless services to children and families. Figure 2.1 shows that legislation and guidance overlap in practice, and Figure 2.2 gives further detail of this.

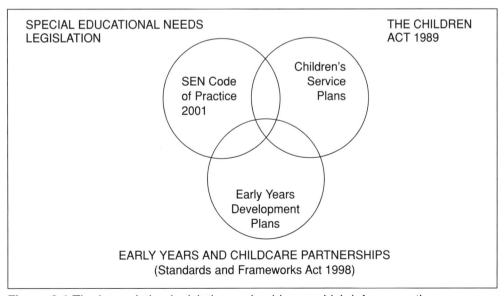

SPECIAL EDUCATIONAL NEEDS
LEGISLATION

THE CHILDREN
ACT 1989

SEN Code
of Practice
2001

Children's
Service
Plans

Early Years
Development
Plans

EARLY YEARS AND CHILDCARE PARTNERSHIPS
(Standards and Frameworks Act 1998)

Figure 2.1 The interrelating legislation and guidance which inform practice

SEN LEGISLATION AND GUIDANCE	THE CHILDREN ACT 1989	EARLY YEARS LEGISLATION
The Education Act 1981: Difficulties now seen as interactive and contextual, not residing wholly within the 'handicapped' child who needs 'treatment'. It is the child's *needs* that are paramount.	Among other things the Act requires the local authority to: • identify children in need • maintain a register of disabled children • provide services which enable children in need to be cared for and brought up by their families • provide services to enable children who are disabled to live as normal a life as possible • publish information about the services that they provide for children in need • listen to the views of children and their parents.	**The Nursery Education and Grant-Maintained Schools Act 1996** requires all early years providers, including private nurseries and playgroups, to have 'due regard' to the Code of Practice for SEN in the same way as schools do.
The Education Act 1993 (Part 3) repealed the 1981 Education Act but retained its philosophy, clarified processes and strengthened its core principles. A special educational need is defined as a learning difficulty which calls for SEN provision to be made.		**School Standards and Frameworks Act 1998 Early Years Development and Childcare Plans.** An early years place, albeit part-time, must now be provided for all four-year-old children whose parents want one. Plans must state the provision available to meet the special educational needs of pre-school children, with the expectation that an inclusive arrangement will be provided wherever possible.
The SEN Code of Practice (2001) provides new guidelines for the operation of the Act (see Figures 2.3a, 2.3b and 2.4). It also places a strong emphasis on early intervention, inclusive education, school responsibilities, partnership with parents and multi-agency collaboration.	A child is deemed to be in need if his health (mental and/or physical) or development is likely to be adversely affected without the provision of services; either direct services for the child or services provided to the family. Emphasis on services for children in need who are under eight, including day care, after school and holiday care. Local authorities are encouraged to support existing schemes.	All registered providers must offer a range of activities within the QCA Curriculum Guidance for the Foundation Stage. A qualified teacher should be involved in all settings providing early years education within the Plan.
The Special Educational Needs and Disability Act (2001) strengthens the rights of pupils with SEN to be educated in a mainstream setting. All schools now have to make clear their arrangements for physical and curriculum access and have proposals to prevent discrimination.	**Framework for the Assessment of Children and their Families (2000)** is used to determine the need for services including early years provision.	**Early Excellence Centres** illustrate good practice in providing a high quality integrated multi-agency early years service.

Figure 2.2 Brief summary of legislation and guidance

Themes of the legislation and guidance

Early identification

> Early diagnosis and appropriate intervention improve the prospects for children with special educational needs, and reduce the need for expensive intervention later on. For some children, giving more effective attention to early signs of difficulties can prevent the development of SEN. (DfEE 1997a)

The increasing acknowledgement that early support for children and families is likely to make the most difference to their future has led to an unprecedented focus on early years education and childcare. In addition to the early years initiatives outlined below, the Sure Start programme has been set up to provide better service coordination, support and guidance in areas where there are more vulnerable families with babies and very young children.

Early years development and childcare partnerships

Early Years Forums represent all early years providers and now include accredited childminders working as part of an approved network. These forums must draw up plans to demonstrate how partnership between the public, private and voluntary sectors will secure a government funded part-time pre-school place for every three- and four-year-old whose parents want one. The integration of early years education with day care and out of school provision is a central feature of these plans which are designed to meet the needs of both children and their parents. LEAs have responsibility for ensuring that children are matched to places that best suit their needs.

All registered early years providers are expected to work within the Curriculum Guidance for the Foundation Stage (QCA 2000). This gives guidelines for teaching and learning Early Learning Goals in personal, social and emotional development, communication, language and literacy, mathematical development, knowledge and understanding of the world, physical development and creative development. There is a specific focus on meeting the diverse needs of children, including those with special needs. Careful monitoring of children's progress throughout the foundation stage, together with the baseline assessment which in England and Wales takes place within seven weeks of children starting reception class, is likely to contribute to the early identification of difficulties and therefore appropriate early intervention.

Registered early years provision is now the responsibility of the LEA rather than Social Services. All services for children providing day care under the Children Act 1989 have been required to be regularly inspected by Social Services departments as well as by Education. This is to become a unified process from September 2001. The OFSTED Early Years Directorate will, among other things, be responsible for looking at the clarity of roles and responsibilities within the early years provision and liaison with agencies. They are also interested in plans for improving the procedures for meeting the needs of individual children and improving partnership with parents and carers.

Early years providers and SEN

All early years providers have to provide information on:

- SEN policies and the facilities available
- staff knowledge and skills in dealing with children who have SEN
- links with organisations concerned with SEN.

They should appoint a member of staff who is familiar with the Code of Practice and able to support other staff on SEN and link with parents and outside agencies.

All early years providers are also subject to the Special Educational Needs and Disability Act 2001. Among other things this puts a duty on schools not to treat disabled pupils less favourably than pupils who are not disabled. No educational establishment may refuse to admit a child because they do not believe they can meet his needs.

The Early Years Training and Development Fund provides funds for initiatives aimed at improving the knowledge and qualifications of all early years staff in nursery settings. This includes training for staff working with children with SEN.

Interactive and continuous assessment

Assessment no longer has an exclusive focus on the child's innate problems, but takes account of the child's strengths and personality and factors within the child's environment. Good practice, therefore, involves assessing the interactions between the child and others, what he is being expected to do, the difficulties he is experiencing, his response to intervention, the strengths he contributes and the contexts in which he is living and learning. Consequently, the emphasis in intervention is not so much on what the child should do as to what should happen in order for him to make progress. Ideally, an agreed programme should identify appropriate expectations, adaptations, activities, responsibilities, approaches, inter-agency and home–school communication, monitoring and review.

The SEN Code of Practice 2001 on the Identification and Assessment of Pupils with Special Educational Needs

Local Education Authorities and schools, including all registered early years provision, must have 'due regard' to the Code in the planning and delivery of services for special educational needs. There is acknowledgement within the legislation that assessment is an on-going interactive process and that an assessment, planning, action and review cycle is an appropriate format for the changing needs of children. The model of assessment as outlined in the SEN Code of Practice (2001) is designed to ensure that assessment takes account of a child's response to intervention.

The SEN Code of Practice: identification assessments and provision in Early Education settings

This sets out the procedures that must be followed. These differ somewhat depending on whether the child is over or under two years. See Figures 2.3a and 2.3b.

A child who is identified as having special educational needs under the age of two is likely to have major health difficulties or a particular condition.

If a parent requests an assessment, the LEA **must** carry this out.

If the child's needs have been identified by others, such as the Child Health Services or Social Services, the LEA **may** carry out an assessment if parents agree to this.

LEAs may carry out the assessment in the way that they consider appropriate. **Statutory procedures do not have to be followed.** Parents must be enabled to participate fully and children should be assessed in a place where the child and family feel comfortable.

Statements for children under two are rare and programmes of individual support should be considered in the first instance, such as home-based intervention. Careful monitoring of these will contribute to assessments after the age of two.

Figure 2.3a Identification and Assessment of SEN for Children Under Two Years

When a child moves into an early education setting a somewhat different set of regulations come into operation. Once the child is in school the terms Early Years Action and Early Years Action Plus are changed to School Action and School Action Plus but otherwise the guidelines are the same (see Figure 2.4).

If a child is in a government funded early education setting which now includes day care, playgroups and accredited childminders as well as maintained and independent nursery schools, the procedures for identifying and meeting special educational needs are broadly the same as for school age children (see Figure 2.4).

If a Health Authority or National Health Service Trust comes to the opinion that a child under five may have special educational needs it must inform the child's parents and the LEA. Such a notification from Health to Education ensures that the LEA monitors the progress of the child. It may, but does not necessarily, lead to a statutory assessment. Health Authorities must also give parents information about local statutory and voluntary services that may be able to help them.

Where a statutory assessment is requested the LEA will assess the evidence that the child's difficulties or developmental delays are such that he requires a multi-professional approach which includes monitoring and review over a period of time.

If it is decided that this is the case then statutory procedures are initiated. These are the same for all children. The contributions of parents and closely involved professionals are of key importance.

Figure 2.3b Identification and Assessment of Children Over Two but Under Five Years

A systematic cycle of planning, action and review to enable the child with special educational needs to learn and make progress.

Early Years Action:

The triggers for intervention are concerns by the child's teacher or relevant practitioner that despite appropriate early years experiences (and provision where necessary of aids for sensory or physical difficulties), the child:

- is making little or no progress
- is significantly behind others of the same age
- has communication and/or interaction difficulties which impede learning
- has persistent behavioural difficulties.

Parents are consulted and if there is agreement that further support is required for the child to make progress staff should seek the help of the Special Educational Needs Coordinator (SENCO). All available information is then collated from early years records, any other agency involved such as Health or Social Services and from parents. If educational psychologists have not already

Figure 2.4 Identification, Assessment and Provision in Early Education Settings been working in the early years setting the SENCO should contact them. Parents should be informed of any local Parent Partnership Services and kept fully informed about their child's needs.

Intervention should be decided in light of the earlier assessment. It may take the form of staff development and training, group or individual support for the child by early years staff or the provision of different learning materials or teaching arrangements. Strategies which are employed over and above the normal differentiated curriculum should be recorded in an **Individual Education Plan.** The IEP should include three or four short-term targets and be reviewed regularly in consultation with parents, ideally at least three times a year.

Early Years Action Plus

This is where external support services are involved to help early education providers. This can take the form of advice, specialist assessments or support for specific activities.

Action Plus is triggered when *despite an individualised programme* the child:

- makes little or no progress in a specific area *over a long period*
- is working at a level *substantially* below children of a similar age
- has emotional or behavioural difficulties which *substantially* interfere with learning
- has physical or sensory needs which require *additional* equipment or regular visits for direct intervention or specialist advice
- has communication or interaction difficulties that cause *substantial* barriers to learning and impede the development of social relationships.

Action Plus is requested following an IEP review. The external support services will need to see records which show which targets have been set, which strategies have been employed and the extent to which they have been effective.

Statutory Assessment. A few children will, despite Action Plus, continue to give cause for significant concern. Parents and maintained schools may request a statutory assessment from the LEA. Other early education providers can bring the child's SEN to the attention of the LEA. In deciding whether to initiate a statutory assessment the LEA will seek evidence about action already taken, how long intervention has been in place and records about the child's SEN and progress. Decision on requests for statutory assessment on children with severe and/or complex needs will rely on reports from professionals most closely involved. Parents' views are particularly important in all instances.

Figure 2.4 continued

The Lincolnshire COPPS procedures

Code of Practice Pre-School procedures are in place for all pre-school children who have special educational needs and are not in LEA/ maintained schools or nurseries. They may be either in early years settings or receiving support within the community. The COPPS arrangement aims to clarify children's needs over time, coordinate intervention and ensure that appropriate provision is made.

Early Years Action is characterised by those people who might ordinarily be involved with young children and their families (such as parents/carers, health visitors, day carers, GPs, playgroup and nursery staff) with the additional involvement of one or more specialist agencies who do not routinely work with all or most children (such as speech and language therapists, portage workers, physiotherapists, occupational therapists, sensory impaired services, consultant medical officers).

Where there is cause for concern about a child further information will be gathered, specific observations made and interventions planned on the basis of these. Review of the plan and outcome may lead to:

- maintaining or amending the current plan for the child and his family
- discontinuing the plan where progress has been made
- moving to Early Years Action Plus.

With parental agreement:

- health workers may refer the child to the Community Health doctor (MO)
- portage workers or Sensory Impaired Service teachers may refer to the educational psychologist (EP).

The aim of Early Years Action Plus is to establish an overall coordination of the interventions into a plan-do-review cycle.

The MO and the EP have regular liaison meetings to discuss referred children.

At these meetings they coordinate and exchange information about:

- the child's needs and learning to date
- current provision – is this effective or should alternatives/additions be sought?
- future implications for education.

They then:

- draw up a coordinated plan which clarifies what each will do
- agree who will consult with parents about proposed actions
- fix a review date.

AGREED ACTION OUTCOMES
A range of assessment and intervention activities

No action ← MO EP → No action
Possibilities Possibilities

Seek more information	Discussions with involved pre-school professionals (Health/Social Services/Education)
Refer to another Health professional	
Review	Home visits
Seek parental approval for direct EP involvement	Observations in a range of settings
MO/EP to give feedback to parents	EP/MO to give feedback to parents
	EP/MO to seek consideration for assessment class placement
	EP/MO to seek consideration for an initiation of multidisciplinary assessment (provide evidence base)

COPPS REVIEW DISCUSSION

These procedures aim to promote good communication and co-ordination between the professionals involved with a pre-school child. They are the link between Health and Education in the Early Years forum. They ensure that decisions are made on the basis of collated multi-agency evidence, that there is minimal duplication, that parents receive consistent information and that actions are regularly reviewed within the SEN Code of Practice (2001) framework. They do not, however, replace Individual Education Plan review meetings where parents and professionals discuss the detail for Early Years Action Plus and future arrangements.

SEN in Scotland

Information here relates primarily to England and Wales. There is related legislation in Scotland and Northern Ireland but details are different, e.g. a Statement of Special Educational Needs in English Law is called a Record in Scotland. The Scottish Office Educational and Industry Department

---

Step 1 Identification of difficulties in learning

The teacher takes action to overcome the learning difficulties within a defined period, generally by adjusting the class programme. The teacher reassesses, making a record of the problems faced by individuals, and their learning strengths.

Step 2 Referral to learning support coordinator

Parents are informed and consulted. Additional assistance may be given to the individual by promoted staff, another teacher, or the learning support specialist attached to or on the staff of the school. Arrangements are made to review progress.

Step 3 Referral to support services outwith the school

Where it is decided that further assistance is required, the head teacher may first seek advice from an adviser or learning support specialist from outwith the school. The next step is to seek parents' permission to refer the child to the psychological service.

Step 4 Consideration of the pupil's needs by the educational psychologist

A course of action is recommended in writing with, where approriate, advice on the content of the curriculum and learning and teaching strategies. Where action is some form of educational programme, arrangements are made for review and evaluation, in consultation with parents and school staff.

Step 5 Consideration is given to opening a Record of Needs

The head teacher, parents and, normally, the educational psychologist consider whether a Record of Needs should be opened. School staff prepare a report on their view of the child's strengths and needs.

Step 6 Medical examination and psychological assessment

The child is assessed. The medical officer and the psychologist prepare reports. Staff in school, meantime, continue to give the pupil assistance.

Step 7 Meeting to discuss opening of Record of Needs

The professionals, including representatives of school staff, meet with parents to discuss assessments. If the decision is that a Record of Needs should be opened, then the pupil's special educational needs are defined and the provision required to meet these needs is specified. School staff prepare or update their individualised educational programme for the pupil.

Step 8 Opening the Record of Needs

The Record is drafted and a copy is sent to parents for approval. Once approved it is 'opened' and copies are sent to parents, school and psychological service.

Figure 2.5 Steps to be taken in identifying and assessing pupils' SEN at the primary stage in Scotland

(SOEID) Circular 4/96 outlines the procedures for opening and managing a Record of Needs (SOEID 1996). There are eight steps as outlined in Figure 2.5. The Standards in Scotland's Schools etc Act (2000) does not specifically address SEN but strengthens the commitment to inclusion and gives both parents and children more say in their choice of school. It also puts a duty on local authorities to ensure there are plans to make free pre-school education available to all three- and four-year old children. In the Children (Scotland) Act 1995 the definition of a child in need includes those who are affected by the disability of another family member as well as those who are disabled themselves.

Inclusion

The term 'integration' for special educational needs which was commonly used throughout the 1980s and early 1990s is now being replaced by the term 'inclusion'. This gives the connotation of being part of something rather than additional to it, and takes account of all children rather than a few. One of the major outcomes of legislation over the last two decades has been the increased focus on the desirability of inclusive practices rather than the segregation of children with special educational needs.

The White Paper *Excellence in Schools* (DfEE 1997c) published in June 1997 states 'there are strong educational, social and moral grounds for educating pupils with special educational needs in mainstream schools'. The SEN Code of Practice (2001) states as one of its fundamental principles that 'the special educational needs of children will normally be met in mainstream schools or settings'.

The Children Act 1989, with its focus on family support to meet children's needs, aims to give children as near normal an experience as possible. Both Children's Services Plans and the Early Years Development Plans must address how the needs of disabled children can be met by services in non-segregated settings wherever possible. The Schools Access Initiative is being expanded so that schools become more accessible to children with disabilities.

Although the SEN Code strengthens parental choice of school it also acknowledges that specialist provision may be appropriate or desirable for some children. Children with severe and/or complex needs are still educated in special schools, albeit with increased opportunities for integration with mainstream peers. Increased links between special and mainstream schools are being strongly encouraged. This will not only support children re-integrating into mainstream school but also offer expertise to mainstream staff to enable them to meet varying educational needs.

The Nursery Education and Grant-Maintained Schools Act 1996 promotes inclusive practices for young children by:

- making it illegal for admissions policies to discriminate against children with special educational needs
- enabling LEAs to make resources available to private and voluntary early years providers to help them meet identified special educational needs.

Partnership with parents

Parental responsibility is given to the child's natural parents whether married, separated or divorced. Unmarried fathers or other adults can only be granted parental responsibility by court order or by agreement under the Children Act 1989. Where there is a care order for the child, responsibility is shared between the parents and the local authority.

Parental involvement, responsibility and inclusion in both decision making and service delivery is an integral part of all the legislation and guidance on special educational needs.

The themes in the SEN Code of Practice (2001) are:

- empowerment: encouraging parents to work closely with schools and local services in order to identify and meet a child's needs as early as possible
- entitlement: to choice of school, involvement in decision making and information about what is being provided for their child
- partnership: all LEAs must make arrangements for Parent Partnership Services which include independent parent supporters
- access to independent conciliation services provided by the LEA to address disputes at an early stage.

The SEN Code stresses the key principles of communication with parents. Professionals should:

- be aware of parents' feelings, their personal investment in their child and the pressures that may be on them
- focus on the child's strengths as well as his needs
- ensure that parents understand procedures
- not make assumptions about parents' ability to be involved
- respect different perspectives
- respect different needs
- recognise the need for flexibility in timing and structure of meetings.

Unfortunately, the rhetoric of partnership has not always been matched by practice. Schools do not always put in place the good communication practices necessary to facilitate parental involvement and there are difficulties at the LEA level because of inherent conflicts within the legislation. Parents naturally want what is 'best' for their child and LEAs have to provide what is 'suitable', taking account of factors that include the needs of other children and the demands on public expenditure.

There is a statutory duty on all schools to publish their SEN policy and make this available and accessible to parents. LEAs also have a duty to provide Parent Partnership Services and all families should have access to an independent parent supporter should they need one. The role of this person is to help parents both with their participation in assessment procedures and when a Statement has been issued. They are there to provide information, clarify procedures and the implication of any objectives. Where required they will support parents at meetings and reviews.

The involvement of children

The Children Act 1989 emphasised the rights of the child to have his feelings known and taken into account when decisions are made about him. The SEN Code of Practice (2001) and the Standards in Scotland's Schools etc. Act (2000) reinforces this principle which is set out in the United Nations Convention on the Rights of the Child (United Nations 1989). The SEN Code suggests that even very young children need to understand that their views matter. They can be encouraged to make choices and share their feelings and wishes with families and staff. This includes being involved in setting and reviewing targets. Consultation with young children may require a range of strategies in addition to verbal communication.

Multidisciplinary and inter-agency working

The need to communicate, collaborate and coordinate has been an increasingly strong theme throughout the legislation and there is now a welcome focus on what needs to happen to translate the theory into practice. There is recognition that collaboration between organisations and agencies needs to be at the structural level as well as in response to individual needs and that links must be formally strengthened between Health, Education and Social Services as well as independent and voluntary agencies. The document *Working Together to Safeguard Children* (DoH, DfEE and Home Office 2000) sets out the way in which joint working arrangements should be agreed, implemented and reviewed.

Within special educational needs there has been a history of fragmentation and competition between departments which at times has led to parents having to coordinate services for their children. The Government accepts that responsibility for improving communication begins with the DfEE's Special Educational Needs Division. There has been a promise to provide information, commission research and disseminate good practice.

The way forward

The needs of children have had an increasingly high profile over the last decade and there is continued pressure on services to raise quality and work more effectively. In response to these various pieces of legislation there has been a concerted effort to improve coordination of services for young children. In many local authorities, provision has expanded with consequent demands for training and monitoring of quality. Partnerships are developing, both with parents and between agencies. Although there is still a way to go, the expectations about the way forward are now clearly laid down.

Woodlands Park Centre of Excellence

Woodlands Park is part of Haringey's Early Excellence Network, comprising three early years centres, two of which were among the Government's first cohort of seven centres of excellence. The centre offers a flexible use of 80 full time equivalent places, responsive to the needs of the community. 15 places are reserved for children with a developmental or family need and about 25 per cent altogether have an identified special educational need. The SEN support assistants are permanent members of staff rather than attached to individual children.

They are part of everything that is going on here, they know the rest of the staff and the parents really well so there is continuity and shared good practice.

The principles of inclusion and partnership are firmly embedded within the policy and practice of the centre. The Head teacher is in no doubt about the advantages of having a community focused provision.

Parents respond very positively to the fact that this is not a stigmatised setting – it helps them come to terms with the long-term nature of their child's difficulties. We have a focus here not just on the child but on the whole family.

Outreach and drop-in services are central to the ethos of the centre. The Deputy Head and SENCO says that it is of great value to families when they can just come in and talk to the person they want to see. Sometimes a chat with a visiting professional is all that is needed and is an excellent use of time. Joint training, sometimes including sessions for workers and parents together, is also seen as a highly worthwhile enterprise and a sensible use of limited training budgets.

The positive, welcoming ethos of Woodlands Park is tangible both for children and their families. The excellence lies not only in the high level of skill and innovatory practice but in the warmth and understanding that underpins all activities and developments. The chart overleaf summarises these.

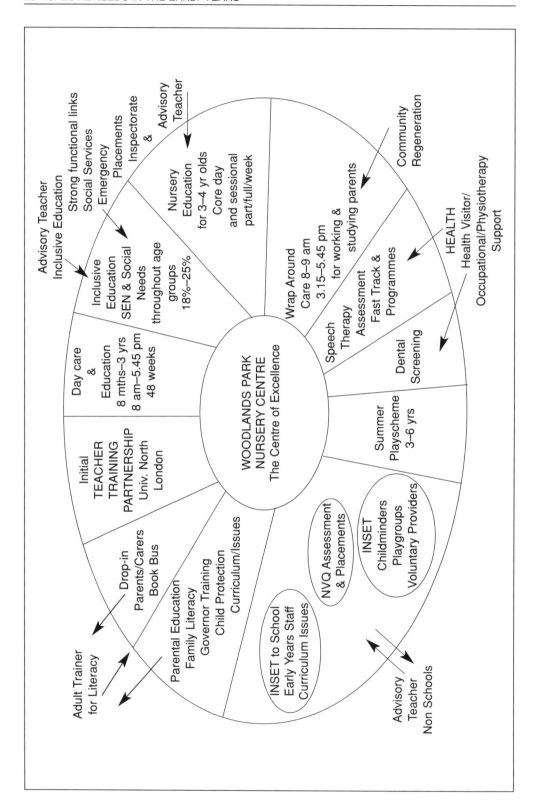

CHAPTER 3

Roles and Responsibilities: Who Does What?

Educational Psychologist
(motivation, self-concept, self-esteem)

Occupational Therapist
(independent feeding skills)

Speech & Language Therapist
(communication,
chewing & swallowing)

Nursery Teacher
(curriculum targets,
social inclusion)

Physiotherapist
(physical support,
positioning)

Professional partners putting together pieces of the whole picture

One of the necessary features of good collaboration is clarity about what different professionals do, how they do it and with whom. This helps to ensure that there are appropriate expectations, little duplication and fewer inappropriate referrals. It also means that everyone knows where to go for specific advice and guidance.

Many services have leaflets for parents that give a basic overview of what can be expected. In best practice, these are translated into community languages. Some services provide open information for everyone about what they provide, how they work and how they can be contacted. Others offer information that is more limited. Inadequate information, however, can lead to assumptions and raise false hopes. Transparency about services, which defines terms and is unambiguous, is usually the best option.

Casework and consultancy

One misconception about how professionals work is the extent to which they will be involved in 'hands-on' casework. Although specific interventions are often necessary, what is equally important is the overall approach and interaction that children experience on a day-to-day basis. The professionals will assess a child's needs and identify appropriate strategies to promote development but they will not necessarily be the people providing all the delivery. Not only do services not have the resources to do this, but interventions are also less intrusive when they happen in a routine way with familiar adults. It is, therefore, likely that the professionals will be consulting with parents and teachers about ways of meeting the child's needs at home and school, as well as offering a direct service when this is indicated.

The discrepancy model

Some hard-pressed services operate what is termed a 'discrepancy' model. This is where a child will be given priority if she has a difficulty which is specific rather than part of an overall delay, i.e. there is a discrepancy between her skills in one area and her skills overall. The rationale for this model is to target resources for children who are likely to make the best use of them. There is usually, however, an emphasis on providing services for the early years where intervention is likely to have the most effect on longer-term outcomes.

Variations in service delivery

Although this chapter gives a general overview of roles and responsibilities, not all services operate in the same way. There continue to be wide regional variations, both in the resources that are available and in the specific activities that are undertaken. We are also living in a time of considerable change and development, with new legislation and guidance in special education, early years provision, Social Services and community health. It would be wise to check with local services for details of how they work in your area.

Coordination within services

As well as improvements in multi-professional collaboration for SEN children and their families, there is also a need for greater clarity and improved communication between different services in the same department. Managers need to consider how all the agencies for which they are individually responsible:

- centralise referrals
- plan together to make joint decisions
- offer discrete services which prevent duplication
- give consistent rather than conflicting messages
- communicate effectively with each other.

This can be illustrated by the different education services who may be offering advice to a school. A head teacher may see an inspector, an educational psychologist, a school improvement officer, a pre-school coordinator, an education welfare officer and a support teacher within a few days of each other. Although the focus of their meetings may be different it would be surprising if there was no overlap. When all these individuals are in different services in different offices and rarely communicate with each other there may be little cohesion in the advice and support they offer. Good practice exists when the various departments have structures which promote collaboration and do not just rely on good will. Some LEAs have gone so far as to create multidisciplinary teams who are attached to specific schools to offer a more streamlined service.

Coordination of services appears to be facilitated by sharing premises.

The real world

Although the aim is for clarity and consistency, good inter-agency work often depends more on positive working relationships than on rigid role definitions. Best practice is where professionals focus on the needs of the child and family, share what has to be done and decide jointly who is doing what. People who are hidebound by their job description may be lacking the flexibility that working with complex situations might need. Planning must be based on what is the sensible thing to do for this child in this situation with the resources and skills that are available.

When people share the responsibilities, the challenges and the solutions, they gain a better understanding of both the pressures others are working under and the possibilities that exist.

More information about the roles and responsibilities described below can be obtained from the professional organisations listed in Appendix 1.

Health professionals

The health visitor

Health visitors are primary health workers for the under fives. They are crucial both in the identification of children with developmental needs and in early support for families. They use the Framework for the Assessment of Children in Need and their Families (DoH, DfEE and Home Office 2000) to work with Social Services to identify children in need. They are also central personnel in the Sure Start programme.

All health visitors are registered nurses and may have a degree in community health.

Health visitors are usually employed by community health trusts, but following the 1999 Health Act primary care groups are taking over as budget holders for their services. They may work closely with GPs and with clinical medical officers (CMOs) in health clinics. There is often a specialist health visitor for children with special needs attached to the child development centre (CDC). This person does not take over from the family health visitor but will support and work with her where necessary.

Health visitors are informed by special care units of any child who is born with a specific difficulty, such as Down's Syndrome or spina bifida. Communication comes either from the paediatric nurses or the liaison health visitor. Local health visitors are also informed about any child who has been admitted into the accident and emergency department. Health visitors are also responsible for visiting families who are new to the area, whatever the age of the children.

At the first home visit, the health visitor will ascertain the kind and level of support the family will initially require. This will depend on many family factors, not just the specific needs of the child. If the baby has a medical need, a paediatric nurse may remain the health keyworker for longer.

Health visitors are jointly responsible for a programme of developmental surveillance. Checks are carried out at the following ages:

- 6 weeks   – carried out by a doctor
- 9 months   – health visitor
- 18 months – health visitor

- 3 years   – health visitor
- 4 and a half years   – doctor

Many difficulties in one or more areas of a child's development are identified at these checks. Records are kept in what is known nationally as the 'red book'. There is also a 'hand-held' record kept by the parent who is given responsibility for taking this to other medical professionals.

Individual health visitors make judgements about the need to refer on, which they cannot do without parental permission, unless this is to Social Services in relation to a child protection issue. If the child needs to be seen by a paediatrician or medical specialist, this must be via the GP or the CMO. Health visitors do, however, make independent referrals to paramedics such as speech and language therapists and other agencies, such as home visiting services.

Health visitors provide a range of support services for families where there are children with a disability or other special need. This may be on an individual basis with the health visitor making regular home visits, by giving information about voluntary groups or by referring to under fives provision or peripatetic services.

When a child with SEN enters school the health visitor will liaise with the school nurse and in some instances may attend an intake planning meeting.

The general practitioner (GP) – also referred to as the 'family doctor'

Every family should be registered with a local GP – often this will be with a group practice/health centre rather than with an individual doctor. GP practices are becoming part of primary care groups. Both GP practices and PCGs are fundholders and therefore act as gatekeepers to specialist medical services. They often have contracts with local hospitals which may limit the choice of where referrals can be made.

Many GPs are now involved in their own developmental surveillance and clinics are held regularly at surgeries. Health visitors may be attached to several GP practices and be responsible for all the children who are registered with those particular doctors. Referral to the child development centre (CDC) will be via the GP after discussion with the Health Visitor or by the CMO at a health clinic. GPs may also refer in response to direct parental concern.

Once referrals have been made and the child's specific needs are being monitored elsewhere, GPs are usually no longer directly involved except with general healthcare and any crisis intervention. Any health specialist who becomes involved with a child should ensure that reports are sent back to the GP/primary care group.

Some family doctors are well tuned-in to current philosophy and practice for children with special needs but others have little awareness of the educational context. This includes knowledge of an interactive and systemic approach as well as the opportunities for inclusion. As GPs often have very close links with families and may be seeing them on a regular basis, it is important to promote inter-agency understanding in order to prevent parents inadvertently being given misleading information.

The community paediatrician/child development centre or unit

Most Health Authorities have a CDC or unit, which is responsible for the assessment of children whose development is giving cause for concern. Some of these assessments will be multidisciplinary. Although the majority of referrals are for children under five, they do see children of any age.

The community paediatrician is the doctor in charge of the CDC. He or she coordinates a team of medical professionals, such as doctors, speech therapists, occupational therapists (OTs), physiotherapists, clinical psychologists, and specialist health visitors. Decision making meetings may be coordinated in the CDC involving other professionals such as educational psychologists (EPs) and social workers.

The community paediatrician is usually the designated medical officer (MO) for SEN. This includes responsibility for:

- ensuring that a child is referred to the LEA if it is considered that he or she has, or is likely to have, special needs which will require special educational provision to be made: the decision making process and criteria for this referral differs within different areas as does the liaison between the CDC, other health professionals and other agencies
- coordinating statutory medical advice, within the expected time limits, for assessment which may lead to a Statement of SEN
- ensuring that all schools have a contact for seeking medical advice for a child with SEN
- considering the pooling of resources between the NHS and local authorities to best support services for children with SEN.

The community paediatrician will also refer on to appropriate specialists as required.

The School Health Service

School Health Services take over from health visitors as the health-monitoring agency for children once they are of school age.

The school nurse

The school nurse works with CMOs as part of the School Health Service. All schools have an allocated school nurse, although the visiting schedule may differ considerably from one institution to another. Often it is the health visitor who will liaise with pre-school provision about individuals, but the school nurse may also be able to offer ongoing support, especially if the child is in a nursery attached to a school.

School nurses are well placed to give specific guidance for all children with particular medical needs, from asthma to enuresis, and to advise staff who will be in contact with these children on a daily basis. Where there are initial concerns about vision or hearing school nurses can carry out basic checks. They may also have initial discussions with parents who have not sought other appropriate medical advice. Along with health visitors they are valuable professionals to include in an intake or transition meeting for a child with SEN who also has medical needs which require awareness, monitoring and/or intervention.

School nurses have knowledge about non-accidental injury and are able to advise teachers on what to look out for and when to be concerned.

As well as monitoring and advising on specific issues, school nurses have always had a role in health promotion. Their brief extends to the mental well-being of children and young people as well as their physical care.

The audiologist

The audiologist is a doctor who has specialised in hearing development and difficulties. Nearly all hospitals where there is a CDC will have an audiology clinic. Children will be referred there if they are communicating well below the level expected for their age. Although this is not always due to hearing difficulties these may either be a contributory cause or need to be eliminated.

The audiologist tests children on 'pure-tone' measures that indicate whether there is impairment in one ear (unilateral loss) or two (bilateral loss). Often, even where there is a difficulty in both ears, there will be different functioning in each. The audiologist will be able to say whether the child has difficulty hearing high frequency sounds (mostly consonants such as 's', 'f') or low frequency sounds (mostly vowels and the less sharp consonants such 'm', 'n'). He or she will also be able to tell how loud the sound has to be before the child can detect it. This information is summed up in a chart called an audiogram. The peripatetic teacher for the hearing impaired will be able to interpret an audiogram and let parents or teachers know what the difficulties mean for the child and her learning. Audiologists routinely refer children to this service.

The audiologist will also be able to tell whether the child has:

- a sensory-neural loss which is an impairment of the internal mechanisms for hearing and may be permanent
- a conductive loss due to temporary blockages
- a mixture of both.

He or she may refer the child for specialist treatment and/or may prescribe hearing aids.

The orthoptist and opthalmologist

Orthoptists and opthalmologists are doctors who have specialised in different aspects of vision. The orthoptist is primarily concerned with functional eyesight, how well the child sees through both eyes (binocular vision) and the muscle balance involved. He or she is concerned with the large variations within otherwise normal eyesight. The monitoring of a child with poor vision would be part of an orthoptist's role, together with remediation such as glasses and exercises to develop better vision. The opthalmologist is more concerned with pathology – the health and disease of the eyes. If the child has a condition that requires treatment or surgery then an opthalmologist would be involved. Sometimes both specialists would need to work together for a child with complex visual difficulties. Orthoptists may refer to educational and other agencies who would be involved in maximising functional vision, but it is very unlikely that opthalmologists would do so.

Child and adolescent mental health

There are behavioural issues for many children with SEN, and a number of different agencies may become involved. When parents are in agreement for a referral to be made to a mental health team or specialist service, they are likely to have already had contact with other sources of support and advice.

A child and adolescent mental health team will comprise all or some of the following:

- a child psychiatrist, who is a qualified medical doctor specialising in paediatric mental health; this person will have responsibility for any medical diagnosis. If any drug therapy is recommended it has to be via a qualified medical practitioner. If it appears there is an underlying medical condition, he or she may refer to a paediatric neurologist or other specialist.

- a clinical psychologist; this person is not a medical practitioner although may have the title 'doctor' following his or her own professional qualification. The psychologist will be involved in assessment, in counselling families and in consultations about the management of the behaviour. He or she may liaise with teachers, and other professionals.
- a psychotherapist; this person is not a doctor. He or she may have trained in working with individuals, groups and/or family therapy. Psychotherapists usually work within a particular model (way of thinking about why difficulties arise) which informs their practice.
- a community psychiatric nurse who will make home visits where appropriate.
- sometimes there is an attached social worker who has a mental health responsibility.

The child and adolescent mental health team may provide all or some of the following:

- clinical assessment, which attempts to ascertain the underlying reasons for the child's difficulties
- individual therapy sessions – with or without parents
- family therapy – where the emphasis is on understanding family dynamics and the meaning the child's behaviour has in this context
- play-based therapy – to allow individual expression, problem solving and aid further understanding
- family support – aimed at management of the behaviour at home and helping families with their feelings about having a child with difficulties
- drug intervention where considered appropriate
- referral to further specialist services.

The speech and language therapist

Speech and language therapists (SLTs) are trained to work with children and adults to assess, diagnose and treat those with communication and some eating problems. They are either graduates in speech sciences or have completed a two-year post-graduate qualification. Many SLTs, especially those trained more recently and those working with children, will have a good knowledge of the educational context, special needs and relevant legislation.

SLTs work with children who have:

- difficulty in producing and using speech sounds
- difficulty in understanding their own language
- difficulty using language
- a stammer or other voice problem
- swallowing or eating difficulties as a result of trauma or developmental delay.

Although SLTs are traditionally employed by Health, an increasing number of those in child services are funded by Education, especially where they are working in special schools or classes or with Statemented pupils in mainstream. They work with parents, teachers and carers, providing advice and support as well as assessment, diagnosis and treatment programmes. SLTs will tend to take an interactive view of difficulties with the aim of promoting optimum communication for the individual child. They have a strong liaison role with other professionals and will often offer training for those working directly with children.

Speech and language services tend to prioritise the early years for intervention and pre-school groups for children with speech and language difficulties are offered by many Health Services. The criteria for admission often depend on the specific difficulties the child is experiencing.

Speech and language services usually have a referral system that is open to parents and professionals alike. Children who are referred to their local CDC for developmental difficulties are likely to see a SLT as part of this overall assessment.

The physiotherapist

Physiotherapists usually complete a three- to four-year degree course and then specialise. Physiotherapists have expertise in physical development and work under a doctor's authorisation. Although most referrals are from GPs, paediatricians and other consultants, some services for children have an open referral system under the guidance of the community paediatrician. A physiotherapist can become involved with a child and her family right from birth. At this stage, giving support to parents is considered as important as giving advice on how to handle the child.

As well as working in clinics, CDCs and special schools, many paediatric physiotherapists work within the home, especially where children are under three. Health visitors may identify the need for a physiotherapist to be involved because of difficulties the child was born with and/or because parents require guidance and support in promoting their children's physical development. Social deprivation may limit children's access to necessary experiences, such as crawling around. Some conditions require physiotherapy treatment to prevent or limit physical difficulties arising.

Physiotherapists need to work closely with many other professionals. Physical development and movement is dependent on vision, hearing and communication skills. Physiotherapists refer to and liaise with home intervention schemes to develop joint early years programmes.

When children enter nursery or school, physiotherapists can advise teachers and special needs assistants about access to play and especially the positioning a child requires to access activities. Where muscle tone is weak children need physical support, and where muscles become rigid children need help to achieve flexibility. It is important that there is consistency of approach between home and school. Physiotherapists can advise schools of equipment they need to purchase, and are sometimes able to provide things on loan. Special schools for physically disabled pupils will have an allocated physiotherapist.

Although there are considerable overlaps between the role of the physiotherapist and occupational therapist, concerns about mobility and larger motor movements would initially be referred to the physiotherapist and concerns about fine motor skills, eye-hand coordination and perceptual skills to the occupational therapist.

The occupational therapist

Occupational therapists (OTs) are graduates and are state registered. Their training gives equal stress to the two components of psychological and physical needs. The central belief of OT philosophy is that activity is central to a person's well-being. An OT is therefore interested in:

- activity as a therapeutic tool
- ensuring that optimum activity is possible for individuals.

The skills and role of an OT are very wide reaching and can encompass such activities as assessment of what is needed to help a child who has difficulty in feeding herself independently to play therapy for traumatised children. OTs are employed by Health Services, Social Services and by some voluntary agencies. Recent legislation is intended to eventually break down the delineation between health and social services provisions.

OTs employed by Social Services assess what is needed to enable someone to carry out the normal functions of everyday living. The outcome of this assessment will be advice, training and equipment, including at times adaptations to the home. In general, if the need for equipment is medical, e.g. necessary for a child's well-being or development, then it is the Health Service who are responsible for provision. If the need is functional, i.e. without specific equipment the child cannot carry out the necessary activities of everyday living, then it is Social Services that are responsible for provision. Equipment solely for use in school is funded by Education and not assessed by a Social Services OT.

Referrals can be made to the Social Services OT team directly by parents or professionals. Social Services OTs liaise with Health paediatric OT services but would rarely visit schools.

OTs who are employed by the Health Service work in hospital departments, special schools, the community and specialist centres. Access to OT services for children who are in mainstream schools is variable.

In some areas, referrals to paediatric OTs must come through a doctor, others have an open system. Although paediatric OTs work with children and young people of all ages, most give priority to children under five years. They are concerned about how a child's presenting problem impacts on function. They are involved with children who have acquired difficulties following accidents or other injury; who have conditions such as cerebral palsy or muscular dystrophy; or who have problems arising from orthopaedic problems, developmental delay, dyspraxia, and specific perceptual difficulties. They may also be involved with a wide range of other difficulties, including children of small stature or other vulnerability whose ability to function normally is affected without adaptations to the environment. Where advice is given to schools, it relates to how a child's motor or perceptual difficulties will affect her learning and the strategies that can be employed to minimise this. This includes how work is presented. OTs may also offer some general advice about specific needs, e.g. developing pencil control.

Paediatric OTs work in partnership with parents and multidisciplinary teams, especially physiotherapists. They often liaise with home visiting services. OTs are likely to become increasingly based within Primary Care Groups.

Education professionals

Apart from teachers and nursery officers, there is a range of different education professionals who are involved with schools. They include link inspectors, school and pre-school support services, EPs, school effectiveness teams and advisors. They have diverse roles in quality monitoring, whole-school development, staff support and meeting the needs of individual children. None of these roles is exclusive and each affects the other. Collaboration between these services to offer seamless support to schools and consequently children is closer to reality in some LEAs than in others.

Portage and other home visiting services

Although portage has been listed under Education, the funding and management of such services varies widely. Some are funded and coordinated directly by Education, others are Social Services based and some organised by Health. Many are jointly funded. Portage workers often work closely with other agencies.

Portage (named after the town from which it originated) is a well established method of intervention for young children with SEN and their families. Portage workers will all have gained the initial Portage Certificate and many will have received advanced training.

The aim of portage is to empower parents to be the most effective teachers of their children. Families are referred through a number of agencies, most commonly through health visitors. Portage workers visit families on a regular, usually weekly basis, offering a highly structured intervention programme. Following assessment, parents agree a learning target with the portage worker. They work together on this and then the portage worker leaves behind an activity chart to record daily intervention and provides related toys and other equipment on loan. Families usually continue with the service until the child has made sufficient progress or is spending a substantial amount of the week in an early years provision.

Other professionals will often make joint visits with portage workers and this may contribute to the action plans for the child.

As well as the basic and advanced training, the National Portage Association provides a range of training courses related to children with special needs, such as quality play courses. This training may be offered to those working in pre-school settings as well as home visitors.

Other home visiting services offer a much less structured input than portage and may see their role as offering more general support and counselling to the family.

The educational psychologist

There is a centralised Psychology Service in every LEA which is available to all maintained schools and early years provision. Educational psychologists (EPs) are psychology graduates with a further higher degree in educational psychology. Most will have had teaching experience. The role of the EP has recently been re-evaluated by the DfEE and there has been a change of focus from reactive individual casework to more preventative work at school, community and local authority levels. In line with the SEN Code of Practice (2001) there is an increased emphasis on inclusion, early identification and early intervention, including assisting schools with the development of policies and helping to develop knowledge and skills for teachers and others who work directly with children. It is recommended in the SEN Code of Practice (2001) that an EP should be consulted when a child's SEN are first identified.

EPs are involved with children from 0–19 years and a significant part of their work is with the early years. They work in partnership with parents, teachers and other professionals. EPs usually make regular visits to provision rather than on a referral basis which enables them to provide consultation on general issues as well as for specific children. This could include devising strategies for managing behaviour, training for working with parents or involving children in decision making. Although EPs may get to know individual families well over time, they rarely work directly with individual children on a long-term basis.

Health Authorities have a statutory obligation to inform Education about a pre-school child who has or may have SEN. The LEA will often ask the Educational Psychology (EP) Service to respond. Sometimes the family will already be known to an EP, but if not further information will be gathered and usually an initial home visit will be made. The EP will usually carry out some informal assessment by observing the child and talking with parents. He or she will discuss the family's concerns and wishes, clarify the involvement they have already had with other services and provide general information about educational provision. EPs give their views about children's needs to the LEA, who make any decision about further assessment and/or provision.

The EP will usually work with others to refine specific programmes of intervention. Should the LEA be asked to initiate a statutory assessment there should usually be evidence that the advice of the EP has been sought and acted upon.

The EP can be a useful resource for both parents and early years workers. He or she will have a wide range of knowledge about aspects of child development, learning and SEN. EPs are familiar with SEN procedures and can provide information about these, the variety of provision and services that may be available and about the processes involved in access. They may also be able to judge the extent to which the child meets any criteria for accessing different levels of support and be able to indicate what are realistic expectations.

EPs often have some first-hand knowledge of the many contexts in which the child is living and learning. This potentially gives them a strong liaison and coordination role between parents, educational providers and other services.

EP Services frequently provide training. Ask your EP Service about what is on offer.

School support teams

School support may include:

- advice and training for particular SEN
- advice about the needs of individual children
- specialist in-school teacher support
- special needs assistants (known by different names in different LEAs).

School support teams have various forms of organisation. In most LEAs the funds are delegated or devolved to schools who employ additional staff or purchase support hours from a central service. Advice from specialist teachers, materials and support for specific activities can be requested from the LEA at Early Years Action Plus or for a Statemented child. The SEN Code of Practice (2001), however, suggests that specialist advice can be useful at an earlier stage of concern.

Some support services are very large, with different teams who are allocated to specific needs, e.g. language team, behaviour team, or to different phases of education. These teams often establish close working relationships with other professionals. The training and supervision that can underpin the work of a centrally based team raises the quality of the support available. The advantage of school based support is that it can more easily be arranged to fit in with the curriculum and other aspects of school life.

An evaluation of school support is central to annual and other reviews.

Outreach workers

Strengthening the links between mainstream and special education has been recommended in *Excellence for All Children* (DfEE 1997a). There is a view that skills that are presently based in special schools should be disseminated more widely and used to promote inclusion. There are various models of outreach work, which may be combined:

- support for individual children and their mainstream teachers especially at transitions
- advice and training

- a resource base within the special school which is open to main-stream teachers
- two-way group or class integration with children transferring between special school and mainstream.

The peripatetic service for the visually impaired

All LEAs should have access to a service for the visually impaired. Many boroughs share a service – a good example of regional collaboration. Sometimes a person with expertise in working with children with visual impairment will be part of a more generic support team. It is often the case that a child with impaired vision will have other developmental difficulties.

Peripatetic services are part of education and staffed by qualified and experienced teachers, most of whom have a qualification as a teacher of the visually impaired.

Services usually operate an open referral system but will require parental agreement and medical information before they become involved. Parents are asked to give written permission to the service so that the orthoptist or opthalmologist can be contacted. In some cases where there are delays in getting this the visual impairment (VI) teacher may make an initial home visit to explain their role.

During an initial visit for a pre-school child, the VI teacher will be doing the following:

- finding out the parents' main concerns
- assessing the child's functional vision – the use the child is making of the sight he does have and the adaptations he is employing
- assessing awareness of light and dark, making eye contact, hand-eye coordination
- explaining and interpreting medical information to the parents in terms of implications for the child and the family
- assessing other aspects of the child's development and needs
- deciding on priorities to help the child develop her residual vision most effectively.

When a child enters an educational provision it is important that the staff make contact as soon as possible with the VI Service, as they are an invaluable source of information and support. The VI teacher will be able to explain the child's difficulties in terms of what it means for her learning and the implications this has for adapting the environment and developing specific approaches. This includes materials, print size, positioning, mobility, access to activities and so on. Some services are a drop-in facility for all professionals involved with children to discuss their concerns in the first instance. Where child protection is an issue, social workers should be invited to all inter-agency education review meetings and teachers to all Social Services case conferences and reviews. The document *Working Together to Safeguard Children* (DoH, DfEE and Home Office 1999) is now being used as the guide to inter-agency arrangements and structures to protect and promote the welfare of children.

Child and family (consultation) services

Known by different names and sometimes run in conjunction with Health Services and/or the voluntary sector, this service offers family support using counselling and therapeutic approaches. It is often used by families who are worried about emotional difficulties their child may be experiencing and/or where there may be problems in managing their child's behaviour. Referral procedures may vary, but where Social Services are the sole organisers, a family may have to be referred by a social worker. Sometimes family support services are offered more informally in early years settings.

Family group conferences are a recent innovation and present a different model of collaboration between families and professionals. They are intended to help families problem solve their own difficulties. Used mostly for families where there is a child in need, they are often set up in conjunction with Health and Education. The aim is to support families in devising family based solutions to problems rather than rely on professionally-led decisions.

Voluntary agencies

Some of the numerous voluntary agencies related to SEN are listed in Appendix 1. Voluntary agencies can be either local or national, and either umbrella organisations such as those campaigning for inclusive education or for specific difficulties. They have a significant and increasing role in the education and support of children with SEN and their families at several different levels. Voluntary agencies may provide, coordinate or contribute to the following:

- information, e.g. publications, conferences, training programmes
- family support, which is usually provided by local groups; these may be generic, e.g. a 'children with disabilities' group or branches of national organisations for specific difficulties, e.g. AFASIC (Association for All Speech Impaired Children)

- respite support, such as Familylink – usually provided in conjunction with Social Services
- individual advice and support; national organisations can give advice for specific issues, Parent Partnership Schemes are usually run by voluntary agencies and can provide individual supporters
- educational provision; the voluntary sectors provide schools or classes, mainstream and special. Several organisations, such as Homestart, provide early years home programmes for general difficulties and others for specific difficulties, e.g. motor impairments or autistic spectrum disorders. Often parents have to contribute towards the cost of this input or seek funding elsewhere.
- LEA policy making; representatives of the voluntary sector are increasingly consulted or even invited to participate in policy making
- pressure groups; these use the media, conferences and other events to raise the profile of the changes that they would like to see
- research and training; major national organisations are often involved in carrying out research activities within the remit of their concerns. Sometimes they decide on areas of investigation and bid for funding, at other times government departments or universities may ask for their contributions.

It is important for all professionals to be aware of local group support for children and their families and to ensure that parents are informed about them. Where voluntary agencies are involved in direct work with children, it is helpful for professionals to liaise. A discussion about the advantages and drawbacks of different approaches will ensure that the parents have full information on which to base their future decisions.

The Voluntary Agencies Directory – from the National Council for Voluntary Organisations (NCVO) lists all registered agencies: Tel: 020 7713 6161.

Summary

This chapter illustrates the wide range of different people that may be involved with a child and her family. Some of these roles are distinct but many overlap. This needs to be seen as a strength rather than a potential source of confusion – but it will only be if people communicate and work closely with each other. This is particularly crucial when any planning takes place. Joint decisions between parents and professionals about who is doing what to support the child, the family and the school must be a first step.

Poppies: Professionals Operating with Parents to Provide Intervention and Early Years Support

Set up by the pre-school service in Newham and run by an early years teacher, a portage worker and a nursery nurse specialising in sensory impairment, Poppies is a weekly group for parents and their children. These children, who have a variety of complex SEN, are welcome from birth until they are regularly attending an early years provision.

Parents are offered a range of multi-sensory play opportunities to help their children develop skills in listening, communication, vision, large and small body movements and social awareness. Professionals introduce the activities as families move round different areas and then encourage parents to take over the interaction, commenting on and interpreting the learning experience. Recording is done together as an integral part of the activity. There is an open invitation for therapists and other professionals to come and join in. Many do so, seeing it as an opportunity to work in a different context with families. Sometimes they offer training or consultation to the whole group.

Margaret, mother of Lauren, a child with Down's Syndrome, is enthusiastic:

> We hardly ever miss a week, it's so nice to come together and you can see little differences in the children. People can be so competitive about their children and here whenever someone does something new it's lovely to celebrate it together.

Abida is a young mother who had just started coming to Poppies. Her son Hamza is eighteen months old and has a serious brain deformity. His many difficulties include severely impaired vision and a specialist teacher attends the session too. This is how Abida felt about it.

> This is really helpful – some of the things I have learnt here I do at home and that really helps Hamza. He likes playing with the other children and now he can focus a little bit he loves the lights and the bright baubles that are hanging up. I see lots of people at hospital and the child development centre but before I felt all isolated being at home. I get support coming down here and seeing the other parents.

After the individual session, there are group activities such as songs and games. Many of these are interactive, to encourage the children's awareness of each other. Everyone has a drink and a chat before going home at lunchtime.

Cyril, father of Brendan, a child with cerebral palsy and West's syndrome, shares information about some SEN computer programmes, and everyone talks about the fun they have had with their children in the soft play room that they visit together once a month.

Newham has a pre-school team comprising teachers, nursery nurses and a senior portage worker. Poppies is one of three groups that are run by the service, which also offers a home visiting service, training programmes, and support for inclusion into mainstream early years settings. Close links are maintained with the CDC and contact made with all relevant professionals on receipt of a referral. Seven languages are spoken by members of the pre-school team, including British Sign Language.

CHAPTER 4

Early Identification and Communication with Parents and Carers

This chapter has three parts. The first two discuss different ways in which children's early difficulties may be identified in nursery or school and the implications this has for approaches to parents. Part 3 looks at some specific issues involved in establishing good home–school communication.

Part 1: Special Educational Needs identified by nursery or school

When reception class teachers or nursery officers begin to have some concerns about particular children and how they are getting on in school, they may wonder if they are right to be worried. Alternatively, they may feel surprised or even angry, that 'no one has picked this up before', especially when the difficulties are more apparent.

Clarifying concerns

The first thing is not to jump to conclusions about a child or act too hastily. Although early intervention is desirable there is no point in intervening, perhaps inappropriately, before there is some clarity about what is needed. Observing the child in different situations over a few weeks and presenting different activities to see how he approaches them will give a lot of information. Watching interactions with other children, seeing how he communicates, the level and complexity of play and doing things with him will give a much better idea of what the child can actually achieve with and without help. It will also identify more precisely the nature of his needs. If a notebook is kept somewhere accessible it is easy to jot down observations and comments without this being an arduous additional responsibility. Over time these brief entries will provide a wealth of information on which to base discussions about the child's needs with parents, colleagues and other professionals.

Avoid a 'deficit model'

It is possible to imagine a notebook containing numerous entries saying things like 'Patrick sat doing nothing all morning' or 'Ayse can't put her coat on by herself'. This may all be true, but does not say anything that helps to inform future action. If an entry read 'Patrick was seated at the sand tray and watched other children play with the sand', you know something about the context he was in and about his learning. If it also said 'When I sat with him to build a sandcastle he watched me. He was unresponsive to sentences but responsive to single words and gestures. He laughed as we knocked the sandcastle down together', you know how he responded to adult intervention and have some idea about the level of his receptive language. Similarly, 'Ayse can bring her coat to an adult and can put her arms in the sleeves if the coat is held', lets you know that she is aware of what to do, can follow a routine and has the physical ability to manage that activity. It is much more useful to think about a child as able to concentrate on a favourite activity for two minutes than to say that he cannot settle to anything at all. It facilitates more constructive communication with parents and others, and also provides a starting point from which to aim for realistic targets.

The learning and behaviour overlap

Although concerns are often raised as a result of 'hard to manage' behaviour this is frequently an integral part of other difficulties. Thinking about behaviour within a special needs framework helps those working with the child to maintain an appropriate professional perspective rather than taking the difficulties personally and feeling de-skilled. Clarifying behaviours for cooperation, independence, attention and play will help to discover whether:

- the child is showing immaturity in most aspects of his development and his behaviour overall is more like that of a younger child
- the child needs more physical outlets for his level of energy
- frustration with communication difficulties is a major cause of his behaviour
- the child appears emotionally distressed – reacts strongly to perceived slights and/or is often angry or tearful
- the child needs positive reinforcement to learn behaviour which is required in school or nursery: he will then especially need to learn that he will get attention by behaving well
- there is a more specific difficulty indicated by 'clusters' of behaviours.

It is easy to quickly attribute behaviour difficulties to poor parenting skills but, as can be seen from the above, there are many reasons that a child might present challenges in a busy classroom. Where parents do have more limited skills or are not coping well they need support, not condemnation. Expectations for the child may need to be changed.

Taking time to accept that a child has a special need

If the child's development is noticeably delayed in one or more areas, the chances are that the doctor or health visitor has indeed recognised that there is a problem and may have tried to address this with the child's parents. They may have actively resisted the notion that their child was not progressing along the usual developmental path, and refused further investigation or intervention.

Some families will not have had much contact with health professionals and little experience of other children. Finding that there is a concern about their child may come as a shock.

Other families recognise that all is not well but prefer a 'wait and see' approach.

When appointments are made without full parental support the family may simply not attend. Their reluctance may stem from having experienced a lack of sensitivity and from feeling blamed or guilty as well as having a struggle to accept their child's difficulties.

Unless there are serious child protection concerns professionals must wait until parents themselves request help for their child. It is useful to maintain a dialogue with the family, however, and hope to facilitate acceptance of the child's needs over time. This will be more likely to be fruitful if everyone is non-judgemental and supports the child and family to the best of their ability in the meantime.

Reasons for denial

When parents have little experience of young children, they may find it hard to both realise and accept that their child is different in some way from others of the same age. In some families, there sadly continues to be a stigma in having a child with difficulties and a lot of effort may be put into not acknowledging the existence of problems, especially within the wider family network. This may also be the parents' way of handling their feelings of grief, guilt and even shame.

In some ways, it may be easier for families to accept difficulties when these are more obvious and visible. Children who have communication and/or social difficulties may have experienced excellent development in most areas until they are about two years old when the difficulties begin to become more apparent. This not only makes it harder for parents to accept there is something wrong, but also makes others less understanding and even condemnatory, particularly about any associated behaviour difficulties.

Parents may acknowledge that their child has difficulties but be reluctant to discuss them for fear that their child will be 'labelled'. They may worry that negative things will be written about him, that these will go on his file, that this will affect how he is seen by others now and in the future and that this may limit his opportunities. It may help to establish partnership with parents if they are initially offered informal meetings to discuss their child's needs, which are not recorded. When these are positive and action-focused, parents may be reassured.

Messages parents receive about their child's special needs

The language that is used by professionals is vital in helping parents come to terms with their child's needs. Words like 'handicapped' and 'backward' are alarming and no longer exist within the special educator's vocabulary. This is because difficulties are seen as interactive and are described in terms of the child's needs. Not everyone is aware, however, of current philosophy and terminology, nor are they always knowledgeable about the possibilities of inclusion. Doctors may, with the best of intentions, give the impression that a child will not 'cope' in a mainstream school when, in fact, this may be entirely possible. Parents may then not always be fully open about their child's needs when they go to register him for a school place for fear of rejection.

The early experiences that parents have in discussing their child's needs can make a difference in how they perceive their child, their child's education and the possibilities for future collaboration with other professionals.

One of the phrases that is in common parlance, by special educators as well as the medical professionals, is 'developmental delay'. This means that a child has a difficulty, which may be long-term. The word 'delay', however, can be very misleading for those who are not familiar with this specific usage. Delay suggests 'catching up' and sometimes this is what parents and even teachers will be seeking – the time when the child is at the same level as everyone else. Children who are developmentally delayed certainly make progress but at their own pace. Looking for an intervention or a level of support which will reduce the gap between their skills and those of other children may be inappropriate and lead to disappointment. The focus must be on seeking optimum progress for each child, and celebrating their incremental successes.

The child entering school or nursery

When the child enters school or nursery, far from 'nothing having been done' there may, in fact, be a lot of history concerning the child's developmental needs. This makes it even more important how the child's needs are raised with parents. Giving them lots of facts about how the child is not managing will only serve to reinforce their fears and anxieties, and this may make it hard for them to 'hear' what is being said about their child's needs and what might be done to meet them.

Approaching parents in the first instance

There are no hard and fast rules as every family is different, but the following format should help teachers or nursery officers to think through their communication with parents/carers, whether there is a significant difficulty or a more minor concern.

Ask to have an informal discussion – perhaps a word at the end of a session. 'Have you got a minute – there's something I would like to ask you?' is better than immediately saying you are worried.

Start the conversation by saying something positive about the child. This is important for several reasons:

- it shows the parent that you are relating to the whole child, not just in terms of his difficulties
- it relieves their anxieties that the child will immediately be 'labelled' or even worse 'excluded'
- it shows some commitment to the child and that you are not only concerned about management
- once the parent's attention is secured there is more likelihood that the rest of the conversation will be heard.

Ask the parents if they have any concerns about their child's learning.

If they say that they do not then you could be more specific, e.g. 'I've noticed that J. seems to need/be struggling with/isn't always able to … What happens at home?'

You could then say something like 'I'd expect most children of this age to be doing... it looks like he needs a bit more help to get there'.

If the parents continue to resist acknowledging the difficulty you could ask them if it was all right if you just kept an eye on the child and we could see how he got on for a few weeks. Few parents could object to this – it is not so different from what would be happening anyway. You then have the opportunity to set up a review meeting.

If the parents are able to say that they also have concerns you may be able to talk more fully about what these are – take your lead from the parents, this may be a very difficult interaction for them. You could ask them if anyone else has mentioned problems to them. If it is appropriate, you may feel able to ask the parents if you could have their permission to contact their health visitor or other involved professional for information. It will be necessary to get this permission in writing, especially for any medical information. Some parents may, in fact, be quite relieved that their own nagging worries about their child's progress are being clarified. They may welcome the opportunity to share their concerns and pleased to know that something is being done.

It is a good idea to end the meeting with a plan of action, even if it is simply gathering more information, finding out more about how the child is doing in specific situations or putting in a minor intervention such as having the child sit close to an adult at carpet time.

A review meeting a few weeks on will ascertain whether there is a concern that requires more substantive assessment or support. At this meeting you could ask how the parents feel their child is getting along, what they think his strengths are as well as the difficulties he seems to be experiencing.

Moving on

If the teacher considers that the child's needs do require further intervention then Early Years or School Action comes into operation. The teacher discusses the child with the SENCO who should also try to meet with the parents to let them know what will be done to help their child.

Although partnership with parents is a cornerstone of special needs legislation, and should be promoted wherever possible, it is not necessary to get parents' permission to put in-school support programmes into place. Parents should, however, always be informed of what is happening for their child in school. Permission is needed for Early Years or School Action Plus and no agency will become directly involved with a child without parental permission. They can, however, give general advice to the school on management for the particular difficulty a child is presenting.

Regular formal reviews of the support that has been put in place will help to clarify strategies that promote progress for the child. These should be regularly shared with the parents so that they continue to hear positive things about their child. Paradoxically this may help them, in time, to accept the difficulties and work in partnership with the school and others. At this point parents may agree to referrals that will access the services of other appropriate professionals.

It is very helpful if school staff have written information about services which they can give to parents, which reassures them about what to expect. EPs and other professionals who are visiting early years provision regularly would usually be pleased to meet with parents to explain their role and answer any queries. Parents may be reassured by this meeting and feel more comfortable about the professional's involvement with their child.

Part 2: Special Educational Needs identified by parents

The previous section looked at concerns that were predominantly teacher led, and the interaction between parents and teachers focused on developing positive communication so that full collaboration could eventually take place.

This section is about concerns that are predominantly parent led, where parents are anxious that their child is not making sufficient progress at school and want teachers to take their concerns seriously. In their interactions with schools, parents naturally want their views to be respected. Even if the teacher does not share the same initial concerns, they need to think about developing a framework in which useful home–school communication can take place.

It is often the case that parents are the first ones to notice that their child is struggling. They may be alerted to this by:

- comparisons with other children
- the child not being able to settle and concentrate on learning tasks
- the child not being able to do the work that is sent home
- the child being unhappy in school
- the child's behaviour becoming difficult to manage.

The early years curriculum

Parents may have expectations of what their child should be doing and learning which may not always be appropriate. This may be because they have an idea of what 'school is for' even if their child is only three. The focus on the importance of early years education may be contributing to parents' anxieties about the development of their child's skills. Where schools and nurseries take the trouble to show parents the educational value of the activities that are on offer this can be reassuring. Parents may not realise the many ways small children learn and the vital importance of play and self-directed activity as well as guidance to develop basic skills. Close communication with parents, not only about what takes place in the classroom but the rationale behind the activities, will also empower parents to support their child's learning at home.

Expressing a concern

Parents expressing a concern may do this in several ways. Sometimes it may be hard to get at the root of what they are trying to say. This could be for many reasons:

- they do not have the same terminology or even the same language as the teacher
- they are anxious, do not want to appear pushy and are hesitant
- they are unsure whether they should be worried or not
- they tend to adopt a certain manner when dealing with anyone they perceive is in authority – this may range from demanding their rights to being very 'respectful'
- the worry they have is complex and they don't know where to begin
- although anxieties are being expressed about their child in school, there are other worries about what is happening at home
- they have experienced a difficult time at school themselves or they have had negative experiences with older children and perhaps feel they have to make a fuss to be heard.

Sometimes parents may start off with a mild expression of concern and become increasingly outspoken if they do not see anything happening as a result.

Teachers might feel that there is an attack on their competency. Although it is hard to see through a negative approach, it is useful, at least in the first instance, to try to focus on the anxieties being expressed about the child. If parents feel that someone is really listening to them they may

'Looked after' children are either 'accommodated' or are the subject of a care order. The first is a voluntary arrangement between parents and Social Services and is usually the outcome of a request for help. Parents must have the opportunity to be involved in all meetings and decisions about their child.

Where there has been a care order the local authority share parental responsibility with the parents, whether the child is living at home or not. There will be a social worker responsible for the child's welfare and this is the person who should be approached to discuss permission for referrals. He or she should be invited to all major reviews and should ensure that Education is represented at any case conferences arranged by the SSD. The social worker will be able to give information about the continuing rights and responsibilities of the child's natural parents and what is appropriate communication with them.

The child may be cared for either in a children's home or in a foster family. If the child is in residential care, it is helpful to establish a close relationship with the keyworker who can then communicate with other staff in the home. Foster carers may be looking after children on a temporary or more long-term basis. Although they do not have any legal parental responsibility they do take the parental role for children on day-to-day matters and communication needs to be maintained with them in the same way as with other parents.

In some more complex cases, a guardian *ad litem* is appointed by the courts. This person has the responsibility for the oversight of major decisions for a child and will report to the court on the child's needs.

Summary

Partnership with parents requires professionals to be non-judgemental, have a high level of sensitivity and pay attention to processes as well as the content of communication. It requires not only interpersonal skills but also organisational structures and policies which ensure that good practice for SEN and home–school partnership is part of the whole early years ethos.

CHAPTER 5

Joint Planning for Children with Identified Needs

Children who have significant difficulties in one or more areas of their development and have had assessments and probably a home intervention programme, may enter early years education with a good level of information available about their current SEN. For most children there will be a continuing need for ongoing assessment to help clarify the best way forward. Small children are developing quickly and continual assessment and monitoring is important for all children in the early years.

Some children with a high level of complex and/or severe needs may begin their schooling in special provision. A number of these children may stay in a segregated setting throughout their school life. Other children may find themselves in an assessment nursery where there is often a high level of staff expertise. Increasingly, however, parents are seeking mainstream provision for their children where they can play and learn alongside their peers. This is especially so in the early years.

There is some debate about whether intensive specialist provision early on will give some children skills to enhance their longer-term inclusion or whether children should be first given an opportunity to learn and play alongside their peers. What is agreed, however, is that all staff should have a good knowledge of the child's needs which enables appropriate approaches and expectations to be made.

Although the law now says that admission policies must not discriminate against children with SEN, the response parents receive when they approach a school or nursery may not be particularly favourable. It will depend on the ethos and value system of the school, the organisational structure and the level of confidence that staff have in being able to meet the child's needs. In some schools, normal functioning is stressed and any different or additional needs are taken in their stride. Where mainstream schools are less than welcoming there may be a fear that the child will take up a disproportionate amount of time and attention, and that support services will not be available.

In some hard-pressed LEAs, resources are certainly stretched to the limit, but even here some schools are much more accepting than others, and more prepared to develop their knowledge, skills and structures to meet the needs of all their pupils as individuals. Inclusive education is a process, both for the child and for the school. There are always improvements to be made, whatever the starting point.

Factors which support inclusive practices

Judy Sebba and Darshan Sachdev (1997) have collated studies that have evaluated practice in inclusive education. Among the factors they have identified which promote inclusive education are:

- the quality of joint planning – especially in relation to the effective use of support in the classroom
- educational labels rather than categorical labels, e.g. reading difficulty rather than Down's Syndrome
- teachers who provide a role model for pupils in terms of their expectations and the respect and value they demonstrate for all pupils
- strategies which raise children's skills in communicating; some children do not cue in to more subtle communications
- teaching strategies which enable all pupils to participate and learn
- pupil participation and learning which can be enhanced by high expectations, drawing on pupils' previous experiences and maximising peer support
- flexible use of support which enhances rather than impedes the process of inclusive education.

Meeting the child and parents

Before any planning takes place it is very helpful for the teachers who will be most involved to have met with the child and her parents. Talking about someone who has become a real person is much more meaningful than having just a name. Even if it raises anxieties about how to meet needs, it will help to specify those needs in the context of the whole child rather than as abstract concepts.

Joint planning meeting

The rest of this chapter is intended to help people think through the needs of individual children and how these can be met in the classroom and beyond. The importance of this initial meeting in school or nursery cannot be over-emphasised for the following reasons:

- gathering and sharing all relevant information
- enabling good quality planning to take place
- handing over between professionals
- valuing the contributions that everyone makes
- establishing good communications
- establishing positive relationships
- promoting a positive 'can-do' ethos
- reassuring parents
- reassuring and supporting staff who will be in direct contact with the child
- addressing potential difficulties early on
- detailing the need for any specific resources from outside school/nursery.

Many parents, especially those who are on their own, appreciate being given the opportunity to bring a friend or other supporter along with them. It not only gives them more confidence, but they are able to talk over afterwards what has been said in the meeting. Parents of children with significant needs should already have been informed of any voluntary agency who may be able to support them and also about the Named Person or Independent Parental Supporter. It is a good idea to check that they do have this information.

Professionals are likely to know each other as colleagues and need to be aware of doing anything that may make parents feel excluded. This includes discussing another matter in their hearing, or using first names when the family are not offered the same option.

There will be a lot to discuss and detailed plans to be made. It is essential that enough time be given for this, although some of the basic information gathering could be done beforehand. It is useful to use a form, such as that shown in Figure 5.1, detailing contact information for those who should attend a joint planning meeting. The agenda of the meeting will need to include gathering of information, general planning, developing an IEP that identifies short-term targets for the child and dates for review.

The participants in the meeting will have the following contributions to make.

Parents will know:

- their child's history
- their child's personality
- what she can currently do at home and what she is just beginning to learn
- whether she is able to settle to one activity or flits from one thing to another
- what she particularly likes to do and/or is good at
- what activities she is not interested in or actively resists
- how determined, confident or dependent she is
- the experiences she has already had and her responses to these experiences
- what encourages, upsets and soothes her
- the circumstances in which she is most and least cooperative
- the circumstances in which she is most anxious or most confident
- other things that influence her mood and motivation
- how she communicates
- how she deals with frustration
- what they have found has worked well in supporting their child to learn.

Parents will be able to give their child's views about things. Even when children do not have language they are capable of communicating likes and dislikes, preferences and anxieties.

Parents will also know about specific circumstances at home and at work that will impinge on their own involvement. Parents may be reluctant to appear uncooperative or to divulge what they see as personal facts and may therefore agree to participate in actions which they are unlikely to be able to carry through. This sets up bad feelings all round. Great care needs to be taken to ensure that decisions are made together and not imposed.

Parents are likely to be concerned about how happy their child will be in school, how she will settle in, how she will manage and learn, whether or not she will be able to make friends and what will happen at playtime. Many parents will be very aware of their young child's vulnerabilities and will be especially protective.

Parents know their child best

Curious

Determined

Loving

Can't hear well from behind

Teachers/nursery officers will share some of the knowledge that is brought to the meeting by parents and other professionals. Their specific expertise, however, lies in knowledge of:

- the developmental needs of this age group
- the educational value of play and other activities for young children
- a range of teaching methods and approaches
- the structure of the day and the week – what happens and when
- the curriculum that is on offer
- what children need in order to carry out certain activities
- the available resources
- expectations for work and behaviour
- the layout of the school – classroom, playground, big halls and corridors
- policies and procedures for a variety of issues
- roles and responsibilities within the school or nursery.

Teachers are likely to be concerned about helping the child make progress, whether they will have the time and resources to do this effectively, where their support is coming from, how this child's needs will affect their ability to manage the needs of the rest of the class and the expectations on them from parents and others.

EPs will know:

- about the interaction between different areas of child development
- what is within the range of normal functioning and what gives rise to concern
- what is needed to develop and maintain a child's confidence, self-esteem and motivation
- factors within an organisation which help to promote communication and a positive ethos
- factors within classrooms which enhance social interaction
- about learning styles
- ways of modifying the curriculum and adapting the environment
- ways of looking at and managing difficult behaviour
- about relevant legislation and special needs procedures within the LEA
- the range of available resources within the LEA, access procedures and criteria
- about any support groups in the locality.

EPs are likely to be concerned that the child is seen as a whole person, not only in terms of her difficulties in accessing the curriculum. They will focus on all the interactive factors within the context of the classroom, the school and the family to ensure that these are taken into account when addressing needs. They will be particularly concerned that everyone has appropriate expectations.

Health professionals will know:

- the child's medical history and identified health-related difficulties
- the implications these may have for learning and development
- any other implications they may have
- what specific health-related interventions have been undertaken and/or may be necessary
- any specialist equipment that may be necessary
- available resources and how to access these
- what monitoring is required
- their own organisational structures in relation to communication with others
- about any relevant voluntary agencies
- what training they are able to offer.

Some health professionals may also have detailed knowledge of the family's medical and social history.

Health professionals are likely to be most focused on ensuring that the child makes optimum progress in their specific area of concern. They may want to know how programmes that they devise and strategies they suggest will be put in place by those in regular contact with the child. Where health workers cannot attend a meeting in person, it is helpful to request written reports from them well in advance. These should give details of their past and future involvement and outline the implications that the child's needs have for their learning. Suggestions for adaptations and/or specific interventions would also be welcome.

Specific areas of Special Educational Need

Each of the following sections deals with a specific SEN. They are structured to assist early years staff and others find out what they need to know in order to plan for the child to have an optimum pre-school and infant school experience. This means ensuring that they have access to the activities on offer and that there are frameworks in place to facilitate social inclusion.

Many children with special needs have multiple disability. For these children early years workers will want to know the answers to questions in several sections. Likewise not all the questions in each section will be appropriate. It may be a good idea to think about what information is needed before the first planning meeting using the checklists provided in this chapter.

Be precise in asking for extra help where necessary

When additional help is to be sought from the LEA, it is useful if schools are precise about how they are utilising their own resources and what they need in addition to these. Asking for support for specific interventions is better than simply asking for someone to be available for so many hours. One of the main criticisms of special needs support is that it is often unfocused and assistants are not always clear about their exact function other than 'being with' the child in question. The focus needs to be on what is necessary for the child to have access to the full learning environment.

Don't panic!

These lists of questions may look very daunting and may make a teacher or nursery officer feel that the task of working with a child with SEN will be overwhelming. The reality is that knowledge can be quite freeing. Understanding more precisely what is required and planning how needs can be met raises confidence. Panic is more likely to set in when people are at a loss to know what to do and have to think on their feet all the time. Planning at the outset how all the adults in the class or group as well as the other children can be involved is a way of reducing stress.

Physical needs

Physical needs could involve difficulties with mobility, with manipulation or with the processes that affect language or bodily functions such as eating or toileting. Communication and self-help skills are discussed later in this chapter so this section is restricted to issues that affect mobility and manipulation. The multidisciplinary meeting should include a physiotherapist and where possible an OT. Where communication or eating is an issue, an SLT should also be present.

Some children have a physical difficulty as the result of an accident or illness. Others will have conditions such as cerebral palsy or spina bifida. Children who have little control over their physical bodies, including their ability to communicate, may have very alert and able minds. Others may have a learning difficulty in addition to their physical disability.

The law now says that all new schools should be built so that all children can have access. The interventions that are planned will depend both on the answers to the questions below and the present environment and resources of the school.

What you need to know

The child's level of independent mobility:

- how well he is able to move without assistance and with assistance
- what sort of assistance is required?
- the child's ability and willingness to communicate his need for assistance
- circumstances in which extra support may be required, e.g. steps, sloping or uneven surfaces
- the child's confidence in getting around on his own
- the sorts of things which might promote his confidence
- does he need additional time to get from place to place?

Is he likely to be vulnerable in the playground? In what ways?

- What might make him less vulnerable?
- Are there any activities that cannot be adapted for him?
- What should happen at these times?
- Is any physical activity particularly stressful?
- What helps to make it less stressful?

Does he get very tired at certain times?

- What is the best way of dealing with this? What happens at home?
- Would arrangements need to be made for him to have a nap at school?

Are there any activities that he particularly enjoys or is good at?

What are the best sitting arrangements?

- If the child has a wheelchair what help does he need to get in and out of it?
- Is there a need for special seating in the classroom?
- How is that arranged and what should happen when the child begins to outgrow this?
- Does he need anything else to maintain a posture that enables him to participate in tabletop or other activities.

Does the child have a difficulty maintaining his balance?

- What assistance does he need with this?
- Does the child have control over his movements, e.g. does he fling his arms out?
- What is the best way of making sure that other children can play with him but avoid flailing arms? What happens at home?

Does the child have a particular strength/weakness in one side?

• What does this mean for presenting activities?

What level of control does he have over the manipulation of objects?

• What helps him to manipulate things better?
• What factors in posture and physical support make a difference?
• What things does he particularly like to play with?
• Is there anything that other children need to know/do to be able to play with him?

Does he need exercises to be carried out at school? How often, how long for?

• Who is the most appropriate person to do this?
• What training is needed for staff?
• Who will carry this out and when?

Does he need any equipment?

• Who will monitor and maintain this?

What interventions have taken place so far and with what outcome?

Are there communication or self-help needs? If so, move on to the appropriate sections.

Self-help needs

Feeding, toileting and dressing are skills that small children are still developing and not all children entering nursery or school are fully independent. It is also not uncommon for children to regress in their abilities when they have had changes or stresses in their lives. Independence skills, especially toileting, often give rise to strong opinions, feelings and potential conflict. In infant schools especially, it appears to cause busy teachers most concern and anxiety. The health visitor and/or the EP will be able to give information about these needs – if the child has difficulty eating then the SLT can also provide advice.

Feeding: What you need to know
• To what extent is the child able to feed herself independently?
• Is she motivated to try to feed herself?
• Does she have any oral motor difficulties, i.e. can she bite, chew, suck and swallow?
• If so, what interventions have been in place to address this?

- Does her food have to be of a particular consistency?
- How does she get food from plate to mouth?
- What help, if any, does she need with drinks?
- Is she independent but very messy? What can be done to alleviate this problem?
- Is she independent but very slow?
- Is it appropriate for extra time to be made available? How can this be arranged?
- Does the child have strong likes and dislikes for certain foods?
- Are mealtimes a source of potential conflict?
- What in particular might trigger this off?
- What alleviates this?
- Are there medical concerns about diet, e.g. is the child failing to thrive, very listless or potentially lacking essential nutrients?
- If so, has the advice of a dietitian been sought?

Toileting: What you need to know

- Does the child have a physical difficulty with his bladder or bowels that means that he is unlikely ever to be clean and/or dry?
- Has the child developed skills that have since been lost?
- Is any possible reason for this known and is it a continuing concern?
- If the child is in nappies how long do they stay dry/clean?
- Does the child indicate when he has soiled/wet himself – how?
- Is he distressed by having a soiled or wet nappy?
- Is he able to indicate the urge to empty his bladder or bowels? How?
- Does he have any level of control over his bladder and/or bowels, i.e. can he 'hold on' for any length of time?
- Is there any pattern to his toileting habits, e.g. needing to go 30 minutes after a meal?
- What do parents currently do at home?
- Does the child use a potty/a child-sized toilet seat?
- What encourages the child to get on and stay put?
- What is considered a reasonable time for the child to sit on a potty or toilet?
- Has there been any attempt at toilet training?
- What was the outcome?
- Is there a need to develop a home–school programme?
- What are the child's present expectations about being changed and washed?
- What resources and facilities are available at school?

Dressing: What you need to know

- To what extent can the child dress/undress herself independently?
- Is she motivated to do things for herself?
- What are the expectations at home?
- Can she manage but is very slow?
- Is this a potential source of conflict?
- What alleviates/exacerbates this?
- Which circumstances in school will require the child to dress herself?
- What exactly will she need help with?
- Is there a need to allow extra time?
- What are the expectations on other children to help each other?
- What are the expectations to try to do things independently before asking for help?
- Is it possible to have clothes that are easier to manage, e.g. velcro fastenings on shoes?

Communication needs

It is estimated that as many as one in five children entering school have communication difficulties for one reason or another. Although specific programmes can be developed for individuals, a strong focus on language development for all children in the early years is essential as this underpins many other areas of development, especially thinking skills and social interaction.

The person most involved will be the SLT. If the child has a social and communication difficulty on the autistic spectrum, the EP will also need to be involved. The child and his family may already have seen these professionals but this is not always the case.

What you need to know

Does the child have a hearing loss? If so, please also see the section on hearing impairment.

Are the child's skills delayed in all or most areas of development?

- Is his language at the same level? If so, please also see the section on learning difficulties.

Is English the child's first language?

- If not, does the child have difficulties in understanding or using the language he hears at home?

- If the child's skills are age appropriate in his own language then he does not have a special need in language development. Many of the interventions for children with language difficulties or delay are, however, also helpful for children learning an additional language.

What is the nature of the child's difficulty with communication?

- Is language normal but delayed or is it disordered in some way?
- Is the communication difficulty part of a wider social difficulty?
- Is the communication causing frustration and challenging behaviour?

Ongoing assessment may be necessary to identify the child's specific difficulties.

Motivation and participation

To what extent is the child motivated to communicate:

- with adults?
- with other children?

Which circumstances/individuals promote this motivation?
Which circumstances, if any, inhibit communication and need to be avoided?
How does the child respond when others make approaches?

- adults
- other children.

To what extent does the child:

- follow routines?
- join in structured activities?
- play meaningfully with other children?

What would be initial steps to support the child's participation?

Receptive skills/understanding

To what extent is the child able to listen?
What are the best ways of gaining the child's attention:

- individually
- in a group?

What is known to be useful in supporting the child's understanding?
Has the child any knowledge of sign language?

- If so which signs are in use?
- Are there any training implications for staff (and other children)?

How much information can the child understand at a time:

- one idea
- more?

What are good ways of checking that the child has understood?

Expressive communication

Does the child have a problem with:

- saying words clearly
- word-finding
- sentence construction?

Does the child initiate interaction with adults/with other children?

- How does he do this?
- How successful are these attempts – with what outcome?
- What are the best ways of responding to the child's attempts to communicate?

How does the child communicate:

- needs
- ideas
- feelings?

Are there words/phrases that can be interpreted by the family but are difficult for unfamiliar people to understand? How can this knowledge be transferred?

What, if anything, does the child use to augment verbal interaction?

What could be encouraged and developed?

What would be helpful for other children to know or learn to optimise communication with this particular child?

What affects the child's level of frustration and how is this frustration expressed?

Which ways of managing this have had some success?

Which communication targets would best help settle the child into the school or nursery?

Hearing needs

Many small children under seven years of age experience conductive hearing loss at some time or another, especially when they have a cold. When a fairly severe hearing difficulty has been identified prior to school it is more likely to be a sensory-neural loss which may be permanent.

Severe and/or frequent conductive loss, however, can affect a child's language and social development, and needs to be taken seriously. In many cases a child with a sensory-neural hearing impairment can have their residual hearing affected by an additional fluctuating conductive loss.

The audiologist and the peripatetic teacher for the hearing impaired will be able to answer many queries about a child who cannot hear well.

Please also see the section above on communication difficulties.

What you need to know

What is the nature of the child's difficulties?

- Does the child have more residual hearing in one ear? Which one?
- What sort of sounds can the child hear and at what level?
- Does the child have a history of fluctuating hearing?
- Under which circumstances is hearing worse or better?
- What does this mean for the child receiving instruction in the classroom?
- Where does the teacher need to be in relation to the child?
- What does this mean for less formal situations?

How well can the child lip-read?
What makes this easier?
Is the child used to hearing aids?

- Are there any difficulties with these?
- Has the child developed any skills in managing these independently?
- How are hearing aids monitored?

Does the child use any signing to support communication?
If so, are there any training implications?
Are there circumstances in which poor hearing puts the child at risk?
How can these risks be addressed?
Has the child had experience of playing with other children?
What helps to make this successful?
How well has the child adapted to these difficulties?
What helps the child make progress?
Are there situations or circumstances that the child finds particularly distressing?
What helps?
Which activities might need specific adaptations or arrangements, e.g. music and singing?
What early years input has the child and family already received?
What are the outcomes from this?

Visual needs

Comparatively few young children born in the UK have severe problems with their eyesight. Teachers are therefore less used to making adaptations for them than they may be, for instance, for a child with a hearing loss. There are many reasons why a child has poor vision, and specific visual impairments may require different adaptations in the classroom. The peripatetic teacher for the visually impaired will be helpful in identifying appropriate responses. Some children will be registered on the BD8 – the register for the blind and partially sighted. Opthalmologists make the decision about eligibility but it is the parent's decision to register.

What you need to know

What is the nature of the child's visual impairment?

What are the expected outcomes for this child – will his eyesight change in any way over time?

How much does he currently see, in which ways and under which conditions?

How has the child responded/adapted to his specific visual difficulties and the use of his residual vision?

What compensatory skills will the child need to develop?

What are the implications for movement around the class and school?

What implication does the above have for learning:

- in the presentation of tabletop activities
- in the lighting required
- in the size of lettering required
- in participating in physical activities
- in creative play – painting, modelling, etc.
- in imaginative play – home-corner, miniature people
- using construction toys
- using computers
- at carpet time
- for stories and reading?

What can be done to help the child integrate learning so that experiences become part of a whole rather than fragmented?

Are there any specific difficulties that need to be addressed in unstructured times either in the class or outside?

How much experience does the child have in playing with other children?

What do other children need to know and do in order to facilitate the child's participation?

Does the child wear glasses?

Are there implications for the use and care of these?

What arrangements need to be in place for mobility training?

General learning needs

Several of the other difficulties described in this chapter will also apply to the child who has an overall learning difficulty, in particular those to do with communication and behaviour. A child who has a developmental delay in cognitive skills is also likely to behave like a much younger child. The greatest difficulty for those working in an early years setting is that young children are often strongly self-directed and within an educational establishment they are often required to follow directions. Some do this quite happily and others are more resistant. Finding an appropriate balance that allows for freedom of choice but extends learning challenges the skills of early years teachers.

Those children who have had, or who are having, an emotionally distressing time may also find it difficult to concentrate, learn, remember, problem solve or play happily with other children.

What you need to know

What are the child's learning styles? Which are being used most:

- watching and copying
- physical – needs to engage the whole body much of the time
- experimental – seeing what happens
- creative/problem solving – making up stories, symbolic play
- listening, asking questions?

What is helpful in maintaining concentration:

- type of activity – which?
- doing things with adults/children
- time of day?

Is there anything that is particularly distracting for the child?

What does the child enjoy doing?

What interest could link in with activities, e.g. animals, a new baby, football?

What else stimulates the child's motivation?

In which circumstances does the child appear to learn best?

Following directions

What supports the child in following directions:

- gaining visual attention – ensuring she is looking at the speaker
- using her name
- standing close to her
- making directions short and simple (but grammatically correct)
- checking understanding
- praising people next to her for following instructions
- praising her for part-compliance
- starting something with her
- reminding and reinforcing
- review and reinforcement (telling her what she has done well)?

Being independent

Will the child do things independently or need encouragement to try?
Are new activities resisted – what helps in introducing different things?
Does the child repeat known activities over and over again?
Does the child need to know that it is acceptable to make mistakes?
Does the child need 'larger than life' praise?
What have parents found most useful in helping their child to learn?
What are the learning priorities for the child?
What are they presently able to do and what needs to happen next?

Emotional, social and behavioural needs

Structured situations are not suited to all small children. Sometimes a child is said to have a behaviour difficulty where, in fact, expectations are inappropriate for his age or developmental stage. Many small children require a high level of physical activity, a variety of activities, opportunities to stand and watch without doing anything active at all and plenty of time to play, develop imaginative skills and problem solve in make-believe situations.

Other children demand a lot of adult attention, which is not easy or appropriate to provide. Sometimes these children have learnt that they can gain attention by behaving in ways it is difficult to ignore. They need to learn to gain attention by positive behaviours.

Some behaviours cluster together and may indicate that the child may be on the autistic spectrum. These behaviours include difficulties with:

- social interaction
- communication
- imagination.

These are usually associated with rigid, repetitive patterns of behaviour and often a fear of unfamiliar situations.

Children who are very unhappy are particularly worrying for teachers or nursery officers, either because they express anger indiscriminately and other children get hurt or because they withdraw from interaction. Some of these children may have experienced abuse, rejection or loss that affects their views of themselves and other people. Other children have simply not learnt the skills they need to cooperate positively with other people and these have to be taught.

Finding out

The most important thing is not to jump to conclusions about why a child is behaving in a way which is difficult to manage, and work closely with the parent to identify the difficulties and how they can best be addressed. The health visitor and EP will be helpful people to talk to.

What you need to know

Does the child have any other difficulties, e.g. with learning or communication?

What are the exact behaviours that are difficult?

How frequently do they occur?

What are the triggers for these, if any?

Is there any pattern to them?

What do parents say about how the child behaves at home?

Which positive activities does he enjoy doing?

What is known to be effective in encouraging willing cooperation?

What soothes the child and has a calming effect?

What does the child say about the way he feels?

What are priorities for the child to learn?

- about himself and others
- to manage the expression of his feelings
- to establish good interactions with other children
- to follow adult directions
- to settle to an activity.

Medical needs

Children may have a medical need in conjunction with a physical disability or other special need. The majority, however, will have a single condition such as epilepsy or asthma. As such this may not be defined as SEN, but does require staff awareness. In most circumstances, the school nurse or health visitor will be able to provide information and advice.

What you need to know

- The condition that the child has, and any educational implications.
- What should be avoided wherever possible?
- What preventative measures/adaptations are helpful?
- What are the signs of any impending attack?
- What should be the immediate response of staff?
- What should happen next?
- Who should be contacted in the event of an attack at school?
- Does the child need medication to be administered at school?
- Where will this be kept and who will administer this?
- How will records be kept?
- Are there training implications? How can these be arranged?

Outcome of meetings

Teachers may feel at the end of the initial planning meeting that there is an enormous amount to do. When a range of issues are thought through at the beginning, however, it saves much time and anxiety later on. Many of the plans and adaptations that make a great difference to a child and her family may, in fact, be quite small and once they are in place they become routine. It is also useful to discuss at the outset how existing resources can be utilised most effectively and, without being negative, give everyone a sense of what is realistic. It is very helpful to know who is going to be doing what and how everything will be monitored. If something is not quite working as it should then there are plans to review and adapt accordingly. It is worth remembering that it is not only *what* happens that matters but also *how* it happens.

The following checklist (Figure 5.1) can be used to help with initial general planning and also with the IEP that sets short-term targets for the child.

- Are any physical adaptations needed?
- What exactly are these?
- What curricular adaptations need to be made?
- Do any adaptations need to be made to the timetable? What are these?
- Is any additional equipment needed? What will it be used for and who will monitor its use? Where will it be kept when not in use?

What specific support is needed from:

- the class teacher
- in-school support resources
- other children

- parents
- additional LEA resources
- others?

What training needs have been identified?

- Who are appropriate trainers and who will make contact with them?
- Who will be responsible for devising and monitoring the IEP?

What continuing communications will be put in place?

- Who will communicate with whom, when, how often and how?
- In particular, who will be taking responsibility for ongoing communication between home and school? What are the joint expectations for this?
- When is the date of the next home–school meeting?
- When is the date of the next multidisciplinary meeting to review progress and needs?

Summary

The joint planning meeting should aim to reassure parents and teachers alike that there is a coordinated team approach to meeting the child's needs. Everyone should have a good understanding of their own responsibilities and the support that is there to advise and help when necessary. Many of the professionals in the team, however, are visitors rather than working on site. It is how the whole school or nursery community also work together in responding to the child's needs that will make a difference to her happiness and progress in school.

Katharine's experience

Michael, who is now six years old, has a specific language disorder and is attending his local mainstream primary school. His mother, Katharine, is very positive about what is now happening for him and has no doubt about what makes the difference:

Its because there is a Speech and Language Service in Education now. Before, when it was in Health, it was difficult for the speech therapist to come into school, there was no exchange of files and I had to take Michael out of school to the clinic. Now the speech therapist comes into school regularly and talks to the teachers. She is able to train up the classroom assistant. We have joint meetings, and I know that there are people in school who are planning for him. I don't have to pass things on from one person to another and sometimes lose half of it in the passing. Now it's like a weight lifted off me, I don't have to worry about him every day he's in school.

Katharine's experience has not always been so positive. Michael had been a very observant baby and had reached his physical milestones early so it was a real shock to discover at the age of two and a half that all was not well:

He was full of energy, and being quite uncooperative. I would say things to him over and over in different ways and he didn't take much notice. I asked the health visitor for some ideas to help getting him to bed and when she came to visit, she noticed immediately that his language wasn't developing as it should. It was really hard to reconcile in my mind; we had been such proud parents. I needed a lot of reassurance and, although they had to be realistic, I was also looking for people to be positive, too.

Following a developmental check and a referral to the CDC Michael was offered speech and language therapy, first individually and then in a group. Soon after starting school Michael was given some support for two mornings a week. Katharine was pleased with the help that was being given but not happy about other aspects of her involvement with the professionals:

All this time I was trying to find out for myself, trying to get information. No one told me about AFASIC (the Association for All Speech Impaired Children) and we had been going to speech therapy for a year before I knew about the local parents' centre, which is very, very good. It's important for parents to have support, not to feel alone. You worry about what's going to happen for your child, you want the best and you don't know what to do. I found out most of what I know about the SEN Code of Practice (2001) and Statementing from a friend who has a child with special needs. People did speak to me about it but I was overwhelmed with it all and didn't understand everything. It's hard to ask sometimes, you don't want to appear stupid but at first you just don't know what people are talking about. Parents aren't professionals who talk about these things all the time, they should be spoken to in plain English and step by step. Parents want to be involved and will be able to be involved; information should be offered and given in a way that parents can understand. I can talk their language now but not at the beginning.

HOME, SCHOOL AND AGENCIES' CONTACT INFORMATION

Child's name_____ Date of birth_____

HOME INFORMATION

Address_____

_____

Name of parents/carers_____

Contact numbers: At home_____ At work_____

Other carers_____

Contact number and/or address_____

_____

Relatives or friends who may be involved

Name(s)_____

Contact details_____

Language(s) spoken at home_____

Community language interpreter

Name_____

Contact number_____

SCHOOL INFORMATION

Name of school/early years provision_____

Address_____

_____

Telephone number(s)_____

Name of school/nursery keyworker_____

When available for contact_____

Name of SENCO_____

When available for contact_____

Agreements for home–school communication_____

Figure 5.1 Contact information for home, school and agencies – *continued opposite*

Record of information given to parents/carers and how communicated

_____

e.g. special needs policy given in writing and explained in meeting with interpreter

AGENCIES' INFORMATION
General Practitioner

Name_____

Contact number_____

Other medical professionals

Name_____

Role_____

Contact number_____

Name_____

Role_____

Contact number_____

Educational Psychologist

Name_____

Contact number_____

When available for contact_____

Education support agencies

Name_____

Contact number_____

Named LEA Officer

Name_____

Contact number_____

Independent parent supporter

Name_____

Contact number_____

Figure 5.1 Contact information for home, school and agencies – *continued overleaf*

Other support agencies

Name_____

Contact number_____

Social Worker

Name_____

Contact number_____

When available for contact_____

OTHER INFORMATION

Special equipment

Item(s)_____

Provider_____

Contact number_____

Name of person monitoring use_____

Contact number_____

Any medication_____

Purpose_____

Administration details_____

Inter-agency and parent communication agreement:

(What information will be sent out, to whom and what are parents' wishes about this?)

_____

_____

Any other relevant information given by parents/carers to be communicated to those working within the team:_____

_____

Next annual or other Inter-agency review will be held on:

_____

Date form completed:_____

Updated:_____

Figure 5.1 Contact information for home, school and agencies

CHAPTER 6

In-School Communication

Ethos, communication and effective schools

There is increasing acknowledgement that the culture of any organisation
is closely linked to its effectiveness. Collaboration and communication are
part of the overall ethos and the whole atmosphere of a school or nursery
is affected by the extent to which there is collegiality. The schools that
are most effective have a culture in which the head teacher has a clear
vision of aims but where everyone takes responsibility for meeting
organisational goals. Where these goals include promoting high
expectations for all children, there will be an incentive to clarify pupil
needs, to work together both within the school and with others to raise
the achievement of all. Clear lines of communication ensure that this
works in practice, information is shared in a regular and accessible way,
people know what their responsibilities are and where their support lies.
Where individual needs are seen as a priority, time and resources are
more likely to be available for planning and review. Where there is an
ethos which focuses on possibilities rather than problems there will be a
more relaxed and positive view of SEN. Where everyone in mainstream
provision takes responsibility for making inclusion work, no one has to
face challenges alone.

Talking with others about a child

Discussing children with other staff members can be very supportive.
People do need an opportunity to express anxiety or exasperation but
communication about children in the staff room is powerful in

establishing attitudes and expectations. A negative framework, which focuses exclusively on what the child cannot do or how badly behaved she is, undermines confidence and promotes self-fulfilling labels. Where a positive ethos pervades the culture of an establishment, this includes the way people talk about, as well as to, children and their parents. This includes the front-line administrative staff who are often the first people to meet with parents or talk with them on the 'phone. First impressions of a school or nursery are powerful and school secretaries carry a special responsibility for the messages they convey.

The Special Educational Needs Coordinator

The SEN Code of Practice (2001) states that a member of staff in all mainstream schools and early education settings must be appointed to act as the special needs coordinator (SENCO). This person has a pivotal role in ensuring that relevant information about children is collated, that appropriate Individual Education Plans are in place and for communication both outside and inside school. The responsibilities inherent in this are central to the progress that children make. Although there has been a wide range of practice in different schools, the role and status of the SENCO is being gradually clarified and this process has been assisted by the publication of guidance from the DfEE. Many primary head teachers, feeling unable to fund a SENCO post, have taken on the considerable extra work themselves and struggled to keep abreast of it. Others have recognised the importance of the distinct SENCO role and have made this a priority within their budgets, even if it is only for a few hours a week. Many SENCOs have indeed complained of not having enough time to do the job properly. The SEN Code acknowledges the demands of the role and suggests that there is careful thought given to time allocation and suggests that the SENCO is a member of the senior management team. The knowledge and skills that are now being developed in schools in relation to special needs are largely due to those individuals who have taken on the role of SENCO with such commitment.

Clarifying roles and responsibilities

In many schools and nurseries, the SENCO is the first point of contact for professionals and the second point of contact for parents, after the class teacher. In others, there remains a lack of clarity about the distinct roles of the class teacher, head teacher, and the SENCO about responsibility for SEN.

This can result in confusion, duplication and bad feeling. Collaboration as a result of policy and planning is good practice – poor communication about who should be doing what is not. It is helpful to work out in advance who meets with parents and when, how outcomes of meetings are communicated to others and the procedures for referrals. Arrangements for providing cover for professionals to meet with key staff can be problematic, and where responsibilities for this are agreed beforehand it ensures that professional time is put to best use.

Although the SENCO has primary responsibility for SEN matters there are often issues which appropriately involve the head teacher. Heads and SENCOs need to agree who chairs and records major meetings, how SEN records will be maintained and accessed, who attends case conferences outside school and how training will be coordinated. It is essential that the SENCO and head teacher meet together regularly to clarify the above, share information and monitor SEN practice in the school.

The SENCO and communication

The communication role of the SENCO is crucial in ensuring that there is good collaboration between school, parents and others. Information needs to be disseminated in a meaningful way to all those who are involved with a child. SENCOs need consultative skills as well as special needs knowledge – telling people what to do is rarely as successful as helping to define problems and strategies together.

The communication role of the SENCO will be facilitated by:

- maintaining up-to-date contact information about carers and all professionals involved with a child – their names, addresses and telephone numbers
- discussing reports from professionals with relevant staff in terms of their implications for the child's learning
- arranging annual reviews well in advance and having them in a block of time to facilitate the involvement of a range of agencies
- having an effective filing system so that information on the SEN Register is quickly accessible and can be updated easily; there are now good computer packages available
- making relevant information about the child in the educational setting available to professionals and others (communication is often one-way, which underestimates the vital on-going assessment role of key staff)
- facilitating meetings between professionals, and key members of staff – possibly covering classes where necessary

- facilitating home–school partnership between parents and key staff
- being available at a regular time for informal discussions with staff
- taking responsibility for ensuring there is effective liaison with support staff and temporary staff
- maintaining and developing a resource base including
    examples of good practice
    training given with dates
    in-school sources of expertise
    information about external agencies, voluntary bodies and support groups.
- ensuring that transitions go smoothly by facilitating the exchange of information.

In *The SENCO Guide* (DfEE 1997b), the role of the head teacher and governors is said to be crucial in providing financial and other support to the SENCO, in enabling her to carry out her functions effectively. At a minimum level, this includes easy access to a 'phone, a desk and storage facilities. The time factor is also an issue that needs clarification with the head teacher and governors. *The SENCO Guide* gives several suggestions as to how to make time available and how best to manage it.

The keyworker

Although the SENCO is responsible for overall coordination, it is sometimes useful for the member of staff who has most contact with the child – or perhaps a particularly special relationship with the child and/or parents – to be designated the keyworker. This might be an early years teacher but could also be a support assistant, welfare officer or nursery nurse. If this happens, the roles of keyworker, SENCO and any other relevant staff must be clarified at the outset, together with decisions about how and when communication takes place.

Clarity, continuity and consistency

Communication with support staff

There are different kinds of support staff who may be involved with a child with SEN. If an Early Years Action programme is in place she may be receiving some additional help from someone in school. If the child is receiving Early Years Action Plus or is Statemented, then the LEA may be funding additional support. This may be support by a teacher or by a non-teaching assistant and could be someone coming in from an outside service. In some LEAs, it is common practice for support service teachers to liaise with the school in determining the role of the special needs assistant and to monitor this support rather than be directly involved themselves.

The relationship between a class teacher and a support assistant can be complex. The following questions may be helpful in clarifying roles and responsibilities.

- How often will the support assistant be in the classroom?
- How will exact days and times be negotiated?
- What is the support assistant there to do?
- How does this fit in with the child's IEP?
- What is the role of the class teacher in the IEP?
- Who decides the day-to-day role of the support assistant?
- What should be the balance between individual work and group work?
- How will the child's inclusion into the class be supported by the assistant?
- Will the support assistant be spending time out of the classroom? How often, and what is the explicit purpose for this?
- What happens when the assistant is not there at the agreed times, e.g. on sick leave or on a course?
- What liaison time needs to be made available for the class teacher and the support assistant to meet together? When will this be?
- How often should regular meetings with parents, the SENCO, the class teacher and the support assistant take place? Who will arrange this?

Communication with lunchtime supervisors

Many children flourish within the classroom, where there is good information about their needs and how best to meet these. It is in the unstructured times of the day when difficulties often arise, particularly at lunchtime. When children have had an unhappy experience during the dinner break, they may bring negative emotions back into the classroom in the afternoon. This does not help anybody. The adults supervising activities in the dining hall or the playground may not be aware of children's specific needs, what it is appropriate to expect from them, helpful approaches to adopt and how they can facilitate social interaction. Both information and skills are needed.

Possible approaches include:

- following agreement with parents, children's individual needs could be discussed with lunchtime supervisors
- the link between behaviour and SEN should be made explicit, together with appropriate responses
- additional training should be provided where necessary.

Tight budgets and contract specifications might mitigate against this good practice but there are ways around this. Here are some of them:

- senior staff provide occasional lunchtime supervision to enable supervisors to have training at this time
- when there is a training day for staff, the lunchtime supervisors routinely have their own training programme; other arrangements are made for staff lunch; money may be available for providing whole or half day training from government funding programmes or other special arrangements
- there is a keyworker lunchtime supervisor for individual children who links with the keyworker teacher or SENCO and then passes on information to colleagues on the child's needs and how to respond to these

- each class or nursery group links with one supervisor so that he or she gets to know the children and the teacher – the children are formally handed over by the teacher to the supervisor at lunchtime; this both enhances status for the supervisor and enables the two members of staff to work more closely together
- training happens 'on-site' during the lunch breaks with trainers modelling inclusive activities with staff.

Communication with supply teachers

Some of the best practice may be put at risk by a supply teacher not being aware of a child's specific needs. Supply teachers may arrive at a moment's notice with little time to give them information. It is useful, therefore, to plan for this contingency in advance. The SENCO and the class teacher can take responsibility together for planning, with the SENCO ensuring that the information is with the supply teacher as soon as possible: it's not much use if it stays in the desk drawer. Where to find this information could be part of a whole-school or nursery pack for supply staff.

The information must be brief and to the point – no teacher coming into a class will have time to read a file! It may be useful to have just one piece of laminated card with four or five points on it, e.g.: Figure 6.1.

SEN information for supply teachers

JAMES (STATEMENTED) has a hearing difficulty – keep him in the front at carpet time, make sure he is looking directly at you. His left ear has better residual hearing.

CARLO (School Action Plus) has support from the behaviour support team on Tuesdays and Fridays. He responds best to a calm, but firm approach. If he throws a tantrum, the other children know to leave him to get over it – if he goes on for longer than a few minutes ask a member of staff to take him to the office. A raised voice makes him much worse.

DELLA (School Action Plus: Statutory Assessment Initiated) has physiotherapy exercises at lunchtime, just needs reminding to go to the medical room before she has her dinner.

SAMI (School Action) New arrival, speaks very little English and is very passive, (learning difficulties?) The class are taking it in turns to play with her. They will be able to tell you who it is this week.

Figure 6.1 SEN information for supply teachers

Continuity

The best laid plans within a school or nursery can be thrown into disarray by a change in personnel. Sometimes there is no chance to prepare for this. If the communication in the school or nursery is good and several people have knowledge of and positive relationships with the children with SEN then this will minimise any negative effects. The SENCO, however, should take responsibility for:

- communication with the member of staff who is 'taking over', however temporarily
- arranging a meeting between this person and any support staff as soon as possible
- communicating with the parents about any interim arrangements
- communicating with the children about the situation in order to reduce any anxiety
- reinforcing peer group support.

Keeping in touch

Sometimes children with SEN have many treatments or illnesses that mean they either are often absent from school or have intermittent long periods of absence. Keeping in touch with such children and their parents maintains good relationships and continuity. A weekly 'phone call is usually welcome, and arrangements for children to make contact is also valuable. This could be in the form of cards or pictures as well as visits. Giving parents some ideas about curriculum-based activities helps to keep the child linked in with what is going on at school.

Child protection

It is sadly the case that children with disabilities and SEN are particularly vulnerable to abuse. All those working with such children need to be aware of this and maintain an appropriate vigilance. Should emotional, physical, or sexual abuse, serious or persistent neglect be suspected, careful monitoring needs to take place. Collated evidence should record incidents with dates, verbatim comments giving rise to concern, and anything else that is worrying. Each school should have a designated teacher responsible for child protection and each LEA will have published procedural guidelines. Teachers who think they have cause to be concerned need to have a three-way meeting with the designated teacher and SENCO to decide on a course of action. This discussion should determine whether a referral to Social Services will be made at this point. Some Social Services Departments (SSDs) have regular drop-in sessions for teachers and others working with children, which provide advice and guidance. It is important to maintain positive relationships with parents as much as possible but it should always be made clear that teachers are obliged to follow up concerns and report any disclosures. As this may potentially cause conflict, any referral should be seen to be made by the school, not by any individual.

Communication with other children and other parents

Communication with other children

Young children do not have the same stereotypes and expectations as older children and adults. They are often able to give children with SEN an experience of acceptance that may put others to shame. They will, however, ask questions and be interested in why their classmate is different. There are a number of ways to address these issues. It is valuable to discuss with parents very early on, about what you might do. Some parents would be very reluctant to draw attention to their child's difficulties and differences. Others are happy for these to be discussed openly. Often children will be able to say for themselves what they would like to happen and how much they want to be part of this. They have a right to be asked.

Ideas for communicating SEN issues with children

With parents' agreement, talk to the class or group about similarities and differences, beginning with the class itself; e.g. some have fair hair, some have dark hair. Then talk about other differences that might mean that children need something extra, e.g. some children do not see as well as others and need glasses. Teachers may then choose to introduce the needs of the child in question.

There are now many books available (some are listed in Appendix 2) which introduce more difficult topics to young children in story form. Reading and discussing these will help to raise issues and answer questions.

Adults with a range of disabilities (but who also have skills in interacting with young children) could be asked to come and talk with children who can then be encouraged to ask questions. Voluntary agencies may be able to put schools and nurseries in touch with people.

Some organisations can provide videos or even live drama groups to raise issues. When given by experienced and sensitive trainers an experiential session can have a very positive impact on attitudes and understanding. This entails replicating some of the experiences that a child with difficulties (usually sensory) may have and what she needs to do in her daily life to adapt to these. This is also very useful for adults!

Sometimes children themselves may choose to tell their story to others and enjoy being the centre of attention. Again, any such proposal should not go ahead without parental agreement.

Communication with other parents

Communication on SEN issues needs to be part of the information that is given out to all parents when children begin school or nursery. An allusion to the school's philosophy on SEN may be useful even earlier, when parents first register their child or even when they make initial enquiries. Written information needs to:

- state the school's SEN policy in understandable language
- outline the commitment to inclusive and anti-discriminatory practices and what this may mean
- clarify how the curriculum on offer will promote the skills of all
- state the school's policy on behaviour including preventative approaches and sanctions
- indicate lines of communication open to parents when they have a concern.

Conflict between parents can, at times, flare up in the playground, often over children's behaviour. Schools may be reluctant to address this directly with individuals but do need to communicate again the appropriate channels for raising issues of concern.

Transitions

Changes often come about because children grow older and move on. These transition periods are potentially difficult, and communication between people at these times makes a great deal of difference to the level of continuity and the smoothness with which transitions occur. People need to be aware that a settling-in period is necessary for both the teacher and the child as they get used to each other.

Between classes

This is usually not so dramatic a change as that between schools. The buildings and staff are familiar and, equally importantly, so are the other children. The overriding need is for good communication with the person who is taking on the major responsibility for the child, usually the class teacher. Ideally, a four-way meeting between the parent, the outgoing teacher, the incoming teacher and the SENCO will provide the following:

- basic information about the child and her SEN
- awareness of any specific vulnerability
- awareness of strengths and any special interests
- information about others involved
- appropriate approaches, adaptations and any specialist equipment
- recent programmes and reviews
- the progress the child has made on past and current targets
- priorities for targets in the immediate future
- arrangements for liaison with parents
- any other essential information, such as other carers, language issues, etc.

If a support teacher or special needs assistant has been involved, they should also attend this in-school meeting. A few 'visits' to the teacher, perhaps with a friend, before the new term starts, may also help with this process.

Between schools

Transition between nursery school and infant school or infants and juniors can be a time of anxiety for teachers, parents and children. Again, it is a question of reassurance and putting the right communications in place at the outset.

The following strategies have met with a level of success; the more of them it is possible to put into place the better.

- The SENCO of the new provision attends a review where the child is presently placed to gain as much information as possible and to meet with the parents.
- The 'old' SENCO opens a file that gives all contact details, desirable outcome or other relevant measurements, copies of IEPs, a Statement of SEN if applicable, and examples of the child's work over time.

- The SENCO shares this information with the child's new teacher(s).
- The new class teacher visits the child in her nursery or infant setting for a morning or afternoon, discusses her progress with staff and ways in which they have dealt with any difficulties.
- The child is given an opportunity to visit her new school, perhaps accompanied by support staff.
- A planning meeting happens prior to intake with parents and as many professionals as possible (see Chapter 5). This could be combined with the final review held in the old provision.

Case study

Hilda, a child with Down's Syndrome, was due to transfer in September, from her infant class to a junior school the other side of the borough. She had done well in her infant school and had been very settled there. Everyone was anxious about the move. During her annual review in March, which the SENCO of the new school was able to attend, it was suggested that maybe a series of visits in the summer term would help with the transition. Hilda had a special needs assistant four mornings a week so it was decided that she would accompany her to her new school for one morning a week for the second half of the summer term. Hilda really enjoyed this and over the seven visits became familiar with the staff, found out how to get around the school and sat in on some lessons with the person who was to be her new teacher. The teacher's worries about being able to meet Hilda's needs were addressed and she became more confident about the expectations that would be placed on her. The new teacher also met with Hilda's parents and established a rapport with them. When Hilda finally transferred in September she was one step ahead of the other children entering the school for the first time and able to 'show them the ropes'. This raised her status and boosted her self-esteem.

The child who arrives mid-term

Sometimes a child arrives in a class with little or no information and within a short while appears to be having difficulties. Chapter 4 suggests ways of approaching parents, but it may be that the child is in this situation because of disruptions in her home life. Many families in temporary accommodation are moved from one area to another before they finally settle. Some mothers may be escaping a violent situation and be very wary of giving out any information. A sensitivity to these issues is necessary but, where parents are agreeable, making contact with any previous educational provision or professionals is likely to be helpful. If it is the case that the child has been on waiting lists for services in other areas then this might be communicated to current services so that she might receive some priority attention.

Children who leave to go on to other schools

Likewise, when a child moves into another area it is valuable if parental permission is sought to transfer information. Offering the SENCO of a new school or nursery an early telephone conversation might help the child to settle in more quickly and have appropriate provision made for her. An educational social worker (ESW) (also known as educational welfare officer) might be involved if the child disappears without any information being given, especially if she is of school age.

Summary

The effectiveness of in-school communication makes a great deal of difference to children's happiness and progress in school. It is not only the SENCO and teachers who are critical in establishing a positive framework but all those who are connected with the school and who come into contact with the child and her parents.

CHAPTER 7

Issues Affecting Collaboration

The first section of this chapter raises some of the structural and organisational issues involved in developing collaborative practices. The second addresses some of the interpersonal issues that impinge on the success of working relationships.

Structural and organisational issues

Working together – from the top down

There are exhortations everywhere for services and professionals to work together in a spirit of collaboration for the benefit of children and their parents. All over the country there are examples of this happening – but it takes time to change traditional ways of working and services may remain fragmented. Often, this 'joined up thinking' has been against the odds and due to the determination of individuals rather than the organisational structures in which people work. Early years partnerships and other government initiatives in Health and Social Services are a real attempt to move in the right direction.

There are a number of factors that will influence whether collaboration and coordination become routine and a reality nationwide. These include:

- government directives and incentives for collaborative practice
- effective liaison between government departments to ensure that the many plans that they are demanding from public services interconnect and support clarity rather than confusion for people in their daily working lives
- understanding by local politicians that joint funding for inter-agency work requires both vision and determination to change fragmented

practices, is beneficial to children and their families and is cost-
effective in the long run

- liaison between chief executives of local authorities and Health
Service managers to develop frameworks for setting joint priorities
and joint planning to meet objectives
- commitment from senior managers to work together at the highest
level. Within local authorities this means that protection of individual
budgets should be secondary to the development of inter-agency
client centred practices
- professionals, and professional bodies, who focus on working
together rather than defending their particular corner of expertise
- the development of a culture in which inter-agency communication
and understanding is given high priority and seen as an effective use
of time
- initial training and professional development that clarifies the contexts
in which different people work and the perspectives that inform their
actions
- joint training and the development of services that provide a
'multidisciplinary team' approach to meeting needs
- the appointment of personnel whose job description includes a liaison
role with other agencies and dissemination of relevant information.

Without the senior organisational and professional will and
commitment implied in the above, collaborative working will continue to
depend on those individuals who are determined to make it happen in
their specific contexts. When they leave, collaboration may cease.

Breaking down barriers in Gloucestershire

Gloucestershire is committed to the development of a more coordinated and collaborative service for families and children with SEN. When a three-year review of Children's Services highlighted a lack of consistency the Education committee of the council had a fresh look at how they could build on their existing good practice to offer more integrated provision. They are supported in this by a parents' initiative called *Breaking Down the Barriers*. Among their many activities this group held conferences attended by both Education officers and Social Services managers. Parents wanted to explain what having a child with SEN meant to them and what it was that they needed.

The council has a joint strategy group looking at Primary Health Care, Housing, Education and Social Services. Managers and fund holders work together on this group to develop good collaborative practice from the top down. An example of this has been the three-way funding of an Early Years Development Officer. Along with providing speech and language centres attached to mainstream schools the LEA is currently funding two speech and language projects in mainstream primary schools. There are already family centres on school sites that potentially give access to many services within a community framework and help promote continuity. The Early Years Development Officer, is keen to build on the opportunities which already exist and develop models of good integrated practice which can lead the way.

The Education Officer for SEN, also shares the authority's vision:

We don't want parents to feel they have to fight a battle – or be passed on from one department to the next. Most of us are in the job because we have the interests of children at heart. We are trying to work together to support families and trust must start from when a child's needs are first identified. We must have the courage to invest in children as early as possible. Rather than an over emphasis on writing Statements we need to focus the resources we have on working in partnership with all sections of the community and neighbourhood schools to meet children's needs. Although flexible and responsive provision is required, we also need a strong commitment within the local community to all of its children. It is important that the school a child goes to has an investment in that child.

Resources

Meeting SEN is expensive. The amount of money available and what it is spent on are of central importance. The answer does not, however, lie in fudging the resources issue. Honesty and clear thinking about the entire SEN budget, criteria about resource allocation and overt priorities give a rationale to decisions. This should promote equal opportunities. The alternative is that whoever shouts loudest wins the resources lottery.

There are no simple answers, but it may be useful to consider the following:

- the more transparency there is about resources, the more accountable people will be for how they are spent. This applies to LEAs and to individual schools and nurseries.
- central joint planning is likely to make better use of existing resources
- the more creative and flexible policy makers and budget holders are, the better use they will be able to make of existing resources
- where joint planning takes a longer-term view, less resources will be required to fund expensive crisis intervention
- where local authorities explore the possibilities for regional collaboration, specialised provision will remain viable and potentially less expensive than other options
- the more joint structures there are, the less need there will be for expensive one-off decision making meetings
- the more emphasis there is on collaborative early intervention, the better the outcomes for individual children – and the more cost effective
- where resources are allocated to developing partnership with parents, the greater understanding there will be about needs, expectations and interventions. This empowers parents to be more effective.
- where the promotion of effective channels of communication is a priority both in and out of school, the more effective each professional and each service will be
- the less duplication there is, the less waste of resources there will be
- the more emphasis that is put on working together, the more supported individuals will feel
- the more supported individuals feel, the more able they will be to meet children's needs.

Time

> Good communication takes time. Services under pressure find that this is often the easiest place to make savings. It may be the most costly. (Ball 1998)

Time issues bridge the organisational and interpersonal levels of working together. Developing relationships, getting to know and understand each other's working practices, clarifying joint objectives and ironing out misunderstandings takes time, at least initially. Making sure that parents do not feel they are being a 'nuisance' means taking the time to listen. Finding out about a child's needs properly does not happen overnight. When personnel are in short supply but the demands of the job increase incrementally, time becomes the most precious resource of all.

Services that experience staff cuts year on year but are expected to carry the same workload will inevitably be less effective. In such situations time priorities need to be renegotiated with senior managers and then communicated to service users.

Time is finite. Demands are not. Priorities need to be made. When initial planning does not happen, time is spent re-inventing the wheel, repeating the same information to different people, having impromptu crisis intervention meetings and generally not putting valuable time to the

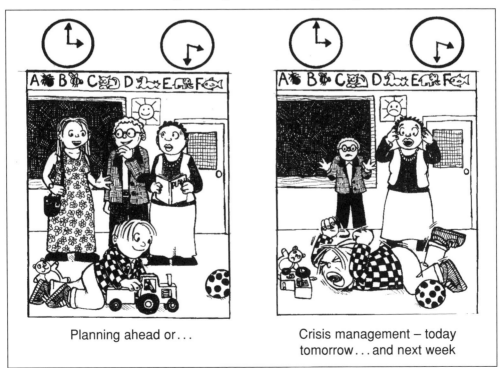

Planning ahead or...   Crisis management – today
                                        tomorrow... and next week

best use. Meetings that are planned well in advance so that everyone can prepare for them are likely to be more effective. When information is kept where everyone knows how to get at it quickly no one has to spend hours in futile searches. When support systems are set up so that everyone knows when other people are available, less time is taken up in chasing individuals. When inter-agency work is seen as productive, practitioners make their attendance at joint meetings a priority. This may save time and effort in trying to make contact with elusive colleagues.

Maybe the real world is not so tidy as this – but there needs to be a will to spend time in planning. There is little point in having a stressed and less effective workforce because the time has not been spent on planning how to use it most effectively. This applies both to the service managers, their expectations of their workforce and the priority they genuinely put on collaborative practices to the day-to-day planning of those who are in regular contact with the child and his family.

Interpersonal issues

Much of the good collaboration that presently takes place all over the country happens where mutually supportive relationships between people are flourishing. Even when structures to promote inter-agency work are in place, these will not thrive unless there is an understanding, trust and value put upon the individual knowledge, skills and approaches of all the collaborative partners. This is not easy to achieve when there are stereotypes, assumptions, professional jealousies and protectionism. Value systems, philosophies, attitudes, expectations and even the language people use all contribute to the success or otherwise of working together. The more people know and understand about each other the more they may be able to look for ways in which they can share the same objectives and focus on these rather than their differences.

Equality

Partnerships are more likely to be successful when there is a balance of power and authority. If one partner is conscious that he has more status or another convinced that her views are right because she has more experience, then any attempt at partnership is immediately undermined.

- Collaboration is not talking to other people. It is doing things together.
- Sharing decisions is not checking out your decisions with someone else. It is making them together.

References

Ball, M. (1998) *Disabled Children: Directions for their Future Care.* Wetherby, Yorkshire: Social Care Group Department of Health and the Council for Disabled Children.

Barnado's (1996) *What Works: Effective Interventions for Children and their Families in Health, Social Welfare, Education and Child Protection.* Ilford: Barnado's.

British Psychological Society, Division of Educational and Child Psychology (2000) *The Professional Practice of Educational Psychologists.* Leicester: BPS.

Children in Scotland (2000) *Guide to the Standards in Scotland's Schools etc Act.* Edinburgh: Children in Scotland.

Cullen, K. (1995) *Multi-professional collaboration? An investigative case study with particular reference to a local authority pre-school home visiting service to families of children with Special Educational Needs.* Unpublished M.Sc. thesis. London: Institute of Education.

Daly, B. and Miller, S. (eds) (1993) *Portage – Providing Quality Services.* Yeovil, Somerset: National Portage Association.

DfEE (1996) *The Nursery Education and Grant-Maintained Schools Act.* London: The Stationery Office.

DfEE (1997a) *Excellence for All Children: Meeting Special Educational Needs* (Green Paper). London: The Stationery Office.

DfEE (1997b) *The SENCO Guide.* London: The Stationery Office.

DfEE (1997c) *Excellence in Schools* (White Paper). London: The Stationery Office.

DfEE (1998a) *Schools Standards and Frameworks Act.* London: The Stationery Office.

DfEE (1998b) *Excellence for All: Meeting Special Educational Needs: A Programme of Action.* London: The Stationery Office.

DfEE (1998c) *Early Years Development and Childcare Partnership: Planning Guidance 1999-2000.* London: The Stationery Office.

DfEE (2000) *Educational Psychology Services (England): Current Role, Good Practice and Future Directions.* Report of the Working Group July 2000 0132/2000. London: The Stationery Office.

DfEE (2001) *SEN Code of Practice on the Identification and Assessment of Pupils with Special Educational Needs.* London: The Stationery Office.

Dickins, M. (1998) 'Forging an Alliance', *Coordinate* **67**. London: The National Early Years Network.

DoH (1991) *The Children Act 1989: Guidance and Regulations; Volume 6, Children with Disabilities.* London: HMSO.

DoH (1999) *The Health Act 1999.* London: The Stationery Office.

DoH, DfEE, Home Office (1999) *Working Together to Safeguard Children.* London: The Stationery Office.

DoH, DfEE, Home Office (2000) *Framework for the Assessment of Children and their Families.* London: The Stationery Office.

Goodinge, S. (1998) *Removing Barriers for Disabled Children: Inspection of Services to Disabled Children and Their Families.* Wetherby, Yorkshire: Social Care Group Department of Health.

Gunner, A. (1997) *The Children (Scotland) Act 1995: Highlight No. 152.* London: National Children's Bureau.

Herbert, E. (1994) 'Becoming a Special Family', in David, T. (ed.) *Working Together for Young Children: Multi-professionalism in Action.* London: Routledge.

HM Treasury (1998) 'Cross-Departmental Review of Provision for Young Children', *Comprehensive Spending Review, Chapter 21.* London: The Treasury Office.

Hobson, K. (1997) 'Educational psychologists and inter-agency collaboration for pre-school children', in Wolfendale, S. (ed.) *Meeting Special Needs in the Early Years.* London: David Fulton Publishers.

Jones, A. and Bilton, J. (1994) *The Future Shape of Children's Services.* London: National Children's Bureau.

Makins, V. (1997) *Not Just a Nursery . . . Multi-agency Early Years Centres in Action.* London: National Children's Bureau.

Mooney, A. and Munton, A. G. (1997) *Research and Policy in Early Childhood Services: Time for a New Agenda.* London: Institute of Education.

Mortimer, H. (1997) 'Surveying professional practice in the early years: multi-disciplinary assessment teams', in Wolfendale (ed.) *Meeting Special Needs in the Early Years.* London: David Fulton Publishers.

National Early Years Network (2000) *Education and the Under-Eights: a guide to the law.* London: The National Early Years Network and Advisory Centre for Education.

North Yorkshire County Council: Pupil and Parent Services (1998) *Desirable Learning for All: Implementing the Code of Practice in Pre-Schools and Nurseries.* Northallerton: North Yorkshire County Council.

OFSTED (1998) *Are You Ready for your Inspection? A Guide for Nursery Education Providers in the Private, Voluntary and Independent Sectors.* Suffolk: DfEE Publications.

Parliament Publications (2001) *Special Educational Needs and Disability Bill* (see www.parliament.the-stationery-office.co.uk/pa/pabills.htm).

Payne, L. (1998) *Standards and Frameworks Act 1998: Highlights No. 162.* London: National Children's Bureau.

QCA (2000) *Curriculum Guidance for the Foundation Stage.* Hayes, Middlesex: QCA Publications.

Roffey, S. (2000) *The Home-School Interface for Behaviour: The Views and Constructs of Parents.* Unpublished thesis. Stratford: University of East London.

Rogers, W. S. and Roche, J. (1991) *The Children Act 1989: A Guide for the Education Service.* Milton Keynes: Open University Press.

Sammons, P. *et al.* (1995) *Key Characteristics of Effective Schools: a Review of School Effectiveness Research.* London: OFSTED.

Sebba, J. and Sachdev, D. (1997) *What works in Inclusive Education?* Ilford: Barnado's.

SOEID (1996) *Children and Young Persons with Special Educational Need: Assessment and Recording.* Circular 4/96. Edinburgh: SOEID.

Stobbs, P. (1998) 'A meaningful partnership', *Coordinate* **68**. London: The National Early Years Network.

Stoll, L. and Fink, D. (1997) *Changing our Schools: Linking School Effectiveness and School Improvement.* Buckingham: Open University Press.

Turner, S. *et al.* (1998) 'Supporting families with deaf children under five: policy, practice and collaboration between Education and Social Services Departments', *British Journal of Special Education* **25** (1), 33–40.

United Nations (1989) *Convention on the Rights of the Child.* Brussels: United Nations Assembly.

Wilson, R. A. (1998) *Special Education in the Early Years.* London: Routledge.

Wolfendale, S. and Cook, G. (1997) *Evaluation of Special Educational Needs Parent Partnership Schemes.* Suffolk: DfEE Publications.

Wolfendale, S. (1997) 'The state and status of Special Educational Needs in the early years', in Wolfendale, S. (ed.) *Meeting Special Needs in the Early Years.* London: David Fulton Publishers.

Index